Drink from the Cup

Drink from the Cup

*

This is a Revised Edition
of the Original
Book.

I pray you will find it useful to read
from God's Word each day in the
Holy Bible.

***

Copyright © Jessie Larman 2020

First Edition: Carnarvon Art Studio 2020

All rights reserved. This book is copyright. Apart from any fair dealing for the purpose of private study, research, criticism or review, as permitted under the Copyright Act, no part of this book may be reproduced or transmitted in any form or by any means, electronic or mechanical, including photocopying, recording or by any information storage and retrieval systems without written permission from the publisher. Enquiries should be made to the publisher.

National Library of Australia

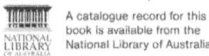

ISBN: 978-0-9872075-8-6 (paperback)
ISBN: 978-0-9872075-9-3 (ebook)
Distributed in Australia and Overseas by IngramSpark

This Book is written so that you may like to read some of these passages and Psalms in the Bible for yourself each day.

To enable you to become more familiar with the words that God has spoken through Jesus His Son and through the prophets of old.

May The Lord Jesus Bless you as you read from His word each day.

January

Psalm: 1 verse 1   Jan 1

> Blessed is the man that walketh not In
> the counsel of the ungodly.....

Try not to listen to the counsel of the ungodly, walk with The Lord. Pray and ask Him what He would like you to do and say today. I pray that you may be pleasantly surprised. Have a lovely day.

1John: 5 verse 4   Jan 2

"And this is the victory that overcomes the world, even our faith"

Remember that we need to have absolute faith in God our Heavenly Father, in Jesus Christ our Lord and in The Holy Spirit. When we have abundant faith we can certainly overcome whatever obstacles come before us each day.

1John: 1 verse 7   Jan 3

Only The Blood of Jesus Purifies us from sin. (The Bible tells us this).

This is true, remember Jesus died on the cross for us as a sacrifice for our sin. We were born as sinful, into a sinful world. When we accept Jesus into our hearts we are washed clean of sin by His blood.

We are then new creatures, we are born again of the Spirit. Then although tempted we need never sin, it does not have to have dominion over us.

Psalm: 3 verse 5 — Jan 4

I lie down and sleep;
I wake again, because The Lord sustains me.

When we sleep our Heavenly Father sees us and looks after us until we wake in the morning. He has appointed angels to guard us. We even have our own Guardian Angel. What a wonderful thought that God loves us so much.

Acts 16: verses 14-15 — Jan 5

The Lord opened Lydia's heart to receive the message of Salvation from Paul. Then all her household was baptized.

Maybe you can ask God to open your heart for Jesus Christ to come in to-day, unless you have already done so. If you have, please pray for all those souls who do not know The Lord Jesus, ask that their hearts be softened to receive Him, even maybe today.

Psalm: 146 verse 7 — Jan 6

> He upholds the cause of the oppressed and gives food to the hungry. The Lord sets prisoners free.

If you are being oppressed in anyway, remember that the food you need is the Word of God. If you become hungry for the Word of God read it. Seek The Lord for your needs today, spiritual food for spiritual hunger. God supplies all our needs, for everyday food and for spiritual hunger. He will uphold you in any oppression - ask and see that The Lord is Good.

Acts: 2 verse 21 — Jan 7

And everyone who calls on the name of The Lord will be saved.

All of us who belong to Jesus Christ were sinners who have been saved. Amen.

Have you ever thought about the above. Never feel inferior to those around you in church because all were sinners who have been saved. Praise God that He sees us as neither male or female when we belong to Jesus. He sees us as we are, redeemed by the blood of our Lord. We are sinners no more, sin has no dominion over us we are all equal in the sight of our Father in Heaven.

John: 16 verse 31   Jan 8

................Yet I am not alone, for my Father is with me.

As Christians we know that God our Father is with us. When Jesus went back to Heaven He sent His Holy Spirit to be with us - to teach, comfort and also to fellowship with us. Where The Holy Spirit is, there also are the Father and The Son. Just think how blessed we are - we are never alone!

Psalm: 94 verse 12   Jan 9

> Blessed is the man You discipline,
> O LORD, the man you teach from your law;

Yes we are disciplined by our Heavenly Father. Often we do not like to be disciplined but it is necessary.

The same as an earthly father teaches and disciplines His children, our Spiritual Father needs to correct us His spiritual children. We have to learn a whole lot of new things when we become Born Again, we have to learn spiritual things and let go of all the worldly ways.

John: 9 verses 1-3   Jan 10

And as Jesus passed by, He saw a man which was blind from his birth. His disciples asked Him, saying

Master, who did sin, this man or his parents, that he was born blind?

Jesus answered, neither hath this man sinned, nor his parents; but that the works of God should be made manifest in him.

If we think about this, surely we can praise God for the things that He allows to go wrong in our bodies, so that we can come to know Jesus through the healing He has received for us on the Cross and be glad that Jesus is our healer. We need to come to know God our Father more and more each day. He wants us to give him praise and thanks for healing us, to know that He is God and He is in control of our lives, that He loves us and wants us to be made whole. We do need to pray and ask, then to receive our healing and thank Him for it.

Ephesians: 1 verse 5 — Jan 11

Having predestined us to be adopted as His children through Jesus Christ, to Himself, according to the good pleasure of His will.

Imagine God loves us so much that he wants us to be part of His own family, when we accept Jesus as our Saviour, Jesus then becomes our Brother and God becomes our Spiritual Father. We belong to the King of Kings, the God of God's. We are very precious to our Heavenly Father.

Psalm: 91 verse 14   Jan 12

> Because He loves me," say's The LORD,
> will rescue him; I will protect him, for
> he acknowledges my name."

Being children of God means that we choose to love Jesus. So as the Psalm say's when we acknowledge His Name He protects us and rescues us from all our iniquities.

Exodus: 15 verse 2   Jan 13

The Lord is my strength and my song; He has become my salvation. He is my God and I will praise Him,....

Yes The Lord is my strength and my song. He is my salvation......I do want to sing to Him and praise Him and thank Him for all the wonderful things that He has done for me, all the blessings that He freely gives afresh each day. Allelujah! Have you thanked Him today for anything, even one little word of thanks to God is a mighty blow to the devil.

Luke: 10 verse 20   Jan 14

"However, do not rejoice that the spirits submit to you but rejoice that your names are written in heaven"

Jesus said this to His disciples, if it applied to them it certainly applies to us. It is marvellous to think that our names as Christians are written in a book in Heaven.

Psalm: 95 verse 6   Jan 15

Come, let us bow down in worship,
Let us kneel before The LORD our Maker.
The LORD God is our Maker, He made us especially for himself, what a privilege to kneel before the maker of the Universe.

Luke: 13 verse 3   Jan 16

I tell you no! But unless you repent, you too will all perish.

Surely it is a small price for us to pay, to repent and inherit the Kingdom of Heaven!

Are you feeling lonely today?   Jan 17

How about submitting yourself afresh to Jesus, ask Him to come into your life even more to-day. Then thank Him for all your blessings and pray with the help of The Holy Spirit.

If you have never asked Jesus into your heart, now is a good time to ask Him to come in.

With God The Father, Jesus Christ His Son plus The Holy Spirit in your life, you will never be on your own again because you are immediately Born Again into God's Spiritual Kingdom. Then let a Christian know that you have done this. Because the declaration of your faith makes it become active!

We who are Christians know this to be true and know that it is good to submit ourselves afresh to God each day.

Psalm: 92 verse 1 — Jan 18

> It is good to praise The LORD and make music to your name, O Most High.

The Lord Jesus and God our Father loves to hear music either by singing or by playing an instrument. If you are not gifted to play a musical instrument then lift up your voice and sing. You cannot say you cannot sing because God gave you your voice and He loves to hear it, so sing in your house, sing in the bath or shower, sing in the car but best of all sing in the congregation.

Psalm: 119 verse 1 — Jan 19

> Blessed are they whose ways are blameless, who walk according to the law of The LORD.

Let us even today try to walk a more blameless life, if we take one day at a time it is not quite so difficult. We can ask The Holy Spirit to help us and guide us today to become more Christ Like. How blessed we shall feel when we have done something according to the law of God and not entered into sin for the day.

Psalm: 121 verse 2   Jan 20

> My help comes from The Lord. the
> Maker of Heaven and Earth.

Thank you Lord God my help does come from you.

2 Thessalonians: 3 verse 10.   Jan 21

..........."If a man will not work, he shall not eat"

This makes us really think, do we truly work for God in all the ways He wants us to. He supplies all our food, all our needs, we are not to be bludgers of our fellow Brothers and Sisters in Christ nor of the world. We are to use the gifts He has given us to work for the Kingdom, in everyday ways and in spiritual ways.

Psalm: 98 verse 2   Jan 22

The LORD has made His salvation known and revealed His righteousness to the Nations.

We need to pray for the Nations that they remember the righteousness of The LORD. The Leaders of the Nations need our prayers so they may govern in righteousness. Today is a good day to pray afresh for all Nations on Earth to come to the knowledge and love of God.

Luke: 14 verse 3   Jan 23

Jesus asked....."Is it lawful to heal on the Sabbath or not?"

If you are not sure of the answer please read the above Scripture. As Christians we do really know that Jesus is our Healer, so let us pray and receive our healing each new day.

Proverbs: 19 verse 1   Jan 24

Better a poor man whose walk is blameless than a fool whose lips are perverse.

We may not be rich financially but how precious it is to live a blameless life. Peace of mind and heart is wonderful to have, so today let us come blameless before our God.

Psalm: 101 verse 1   Jan 25

I will sing of Your love and justice; to You, O LORD, I will sing praise.

It is lovely to sing praises to The LORD our God and to Jesus. Have you ever asked The Holy Spirit to help you sing. He is so lovely, He loves singing, even quietly in our own prayer time we can ask Him to be with our singing.

Exodus: 15 verse 2   Jan 26

The Lord is my strength and my song; He has become my salvation. He is my God and I will praise Him.......

Yes you are my God and I will praise you. Thank you Heavenly Father for all your love towards me.

Ephesians: 1 verse 3   Jan 27

Praise be to the God and Father of our Lord Jesus Christ, who has blessed us in the heavenly realms with every spiritual blessing in Christ.

Can you ever imagine all the beautiful spiritual blessings that we have been given? Just sit and think for a moment on some of them - then what about the earthly blessings that we have. God loves us so much.

He really wants us to have the best of His blessings. I wonder what special blessing is in store for us today?

Psalm: 97 verse 10　　　　　　　　　　Jan 28

Let those who love The LORD hate evil, for
He guards the lives of His faithful ones and
delivers them from the hand of the wicked.
Thank you LORD for your protection
toward me and my family including all those
I love and pray for.
Amen.

John: 1 verse 12　　　　　　　　　　Jan 29

But as many as received Him, to them gave He power to become the sons of God, even to them that believe on His Name:

We must believe on and in the name of Jesus, then we can become sons of God filled with all power and authority of Jesus Christ our Lord. With the knowledge that God is truly Our Father in Heaven.

Psalm: 4 verse 4.　　　　　　　　　　Jan 30

In your anger do not sin,

Remember we all get angry at times but even though we are angry with something or someone it is still not a signal to sin. We are not to become violent or nasty to anyone, if we do become angry we must repent, ask Jesus to forgive us our anger and continue to serve in the love of The Lord. - Then feel the peace of The Lord when Jesus forgives us.

Luke: 4 verse 1   Jan 31

Jesus, full of the Holy Spirit, returned from the Jordan and was led by The Spirit in the desert,

Just think for a moment, have you ever been tempted by the devil? You may have been led into the desert, that could be a place where you have said - where are you God. A place where you have felt so alone.

Remember, Jesus was tempted in the desert but He did not give Himself over to the devils ways. Neither must we, these are the times that we learn more about God and when we come out of that desert experience how much stronger in The Lord we are. Times of testing are of The Lord, to strengthen our character and show that we put our trust in Him. So praise God, thank Him for your blessings. Then you will come out of the desert quicker than you ever thought possible.

The Lords Prayer.

Our Father who art in Heaven,
Hallowed be your Name.
Your Kingdom come. Your Will be done.
On Earth as it is in Heaven. Give
us today our daily bread.
And forgive us our Trespasses, as we
forgive those who sin against us.
Lead us not into Temptation. But
Deliver us from evil. For Yours is
the Kingdom, The Power and The
Glory, For Ever and Ever - Amen.

This is the Prayer that Jesus taught
His Disciples to Pray.
You will find it in:
St. Luke Chapter 11 verse 2
In your Holy Bible.

***

Drink from the Cup of Living Water.
God's Word from the Holy Bible.

February

Psalm: 119 Verse 32 — Feb 1

> I run the path of your commands,
> for you have set my heart free.

LORD you have set my heart free, free to love The Lord Jesus and to serve Him. I love your commands, one which asks me to walk a blameless life. Please God our Heavenly Father help me to do this today with the guidance of your Holy Spirit. Amen.

Nehemiah: 1 verses 10-11 — Feb 2

They are your servants and your people, whom you redeemed by your great strength and your mighty hand. O Lord, let your ear be attentive to the prayer of this your servant and to the prayer of your servants who delight in revering your name................

Please hear my prayer today Lord God, I am one of your servants who delights in revering your name.

And I know that the Name of Jesus your Son is the Name above all names on this earth where I am living now.

Proverbs: 31 verse 30 — Feb 3

> Charm is deceptive and beauty is fleeting;
> But a woman who fears The LORD is to be praised.

I like to think that this Scripture applies to all Mankind. We know that you are an awesome God.

It is a Holy Fear that you want us to have, not that we should be frightened of you because you are the God of Love and in perfect love there is no fear. So if there is no deceit in our hearts then we may be praised and will be able to give to you all the Glory that you desire from us. So may my beauty be in knowing you today and forever more. Amen.

2 John: 1 verse 6   Feb 4

And this is love: that we walk in obedience to His commands. As you have heard from the beginning, His command is that you walk in love.

As we read yesterday you are a God of Love and to love you means just what the above verse says - that we walk in obedience to your ways. We can only do that when we have invited Jesus into our lives and we live in your Kingdom on this earth. Praise you Heavenly Father that you enable us to walk in obedience today.

Isaiah: 30 verse 18   Feb 5

Yet The LORD longs to be gracious to you; He rises to show you compassion. For The LORD is a God of justice. Blessed are all who wait for Him!

Thank you LORD that you are a God of compassion please continue to have compassion on me and my family, especially today. Thank you for all your blessings to me. Amen.

Psalm: 3 verse 5 — Feb 6

> I lie down and sleep; I wake again,
> because The LORD sustains me.

Because I know that The LORD has His Holy Angels looking after me, I can sleep in peace. Please know that when we belong to God He has charge over us.

Psalm: 96 verse 9 — Feb 7

> Worship The LORD in the splendour of His
> holiness; tremble before Him, all the earth.

How can we ever imagine the splendour of His holiness; He must be so beautiful surrounded by glory and Angels, singing and serving Him in Heaven. No wonder the whole earth shall tremble before Him. And yet He has given to us His Son Jesus, who intercedes for those of us who have accepted Jesus as our Saviour. So we need never tremble in fear of God our Heavenly Father, we can worship Him in the splendour of His holiness.

Feb 8

If someone accused you of being a Christian—would there be enough evidence to prove that you are one?

Don't be offended by the above, think quietly a moment to understand what it means. i.e. is there enough evidence in our every day living to show that we belong to Gods Kingdom? Do we speak and act lovingly towards others each day, not just when we feel like it! - What evidence can we show today? Can we forgive, are we walking in truth and righteousness?

Psalm: 100 verse 3   Feb 9

> Know that The LORD is God.
> It is He who made us and we are His, we are
> His people, the sheep of His pasture.

It's incredible to know that we have a Shepherd, who cares enough for us, that He sent His only Son Jesus to be slain on the Cross as a Sheep without blemish for our sins. Let _us_ try to be sheep without a blemish.

Shall we start afresh today?

John: 14 verse 6   Feb 10

Jesus answered, "I am the way and the truth and the life. No-one comes to The Father except through me."

No other religion anywhere can go to God our Father in Heaven unless they accept Jesus Christ as Lord. We must invite Jesus into our hearts for our own spirit in us to be Born Again into the Kingdom of God. I praise The Lord that I have done that, what about yourself, remember today is a good day, if you have not already done so.

John: 13 verse 34   Feb 11

"A new command I give you: Love one another. As I have loved you, so you must love one another."

Do we really love one another with the love of the Lord Jesus. It's very difficult sometimes isn't it? But you know, we do have to try and when we make that special effort to try to love or care for some whom we are not too keen on, or are not getting on with very well, it is amazing what The Lord can do if we ask for His help. Give it a try - ask He say's and you shall receive.

Ephesians: 4 verse 1   Feb 12

As a prisoner for The Lord, then I urge you to live a life worthy of the calling you have received.

What a wonderful thing it is when God Himself has called us into His Kingdom. What an honour to be a prisoner for Jesus. It's only with His help that we can ever be truly worthy of the calling we have received to work for the Kingdom of God.

Romans: 1 verse 16   Feb 13

For I am not ashamed of the Gospel of Christ.

I pray that we too are not ashamed of the Gospel of Christ. That we will speak to unbelievers about Jesus and not be embarrassed or ashamed to mention His Name and tell them what He has done for us.

Psalm: 99 verse 1   Feb 14

The LORD reigns, let the Nations tremble; He sits enthroned between the cherubim, let the earth shake.

The LORD God does indeed reign, Praise The LORD that He does, where would we be if He did not reign. It does not bear thinking about. So let us praise Him today that He is in charge of our lives.

I praise you LORD God that you are in charge of my life now and forever and ever. Amen.

Isaiah: 58 verse 11   Feb 15

The LORD shall guide thee continually and satisfy thy soul in drought and make fat thy bones; and thou shalt be like a watered garden and like a spring of water, whose waters fail not.

Wouldn't it be lovely if we didn't fail The LORD today, let us ask The Holy Spirit to help us to pray that we can be beautiful like a watered garden full of freshness and perfume that will rise to Him in the Heavenlies.

1 Corinthians: 13 verse 3   Feb 16

"A new command I give you: Love one another. As I have loved you, so you must love one another."

If I give all I possess to the poor and surrender my body to the flames but have not love, I gain nothing.

We as humans cannot possibly live to the full without love. As you read the above chapter I pray that The Lord Jesus will guide you into greater understanding regarding the facts about love. It is one of the most beautiful and powerful chapters in the Bible. Without His love and the love of God we truly are nothing.

> Does God hold The
> KEY TO YOUR
> Heart?

Psalm: 7 verse 10   Feb 17

> My shield is God Most High, who
> saves the upright in heart.

When our heart is right with God He truly is our shield against the devil and all his ways. We best watch out on the occasions when our heart is not right toward God. That is when sin can enter in and God will not be our shield to stop it entering. Today let us try to be right in our hearts and in our thinking.

Isaiah: 32 verses 15-16   Feb 18

Until the Spirit is poured upon us from on high and the desert becomes a fertile field and the fertile field seems like a forest. Justice will dwell in the desert and righteousness live in the fertile field.

Praise The Lord that He pours out His Spirit upon us without measure when we ask of Him and walk in obedience to God our Father. We too can then become like a fertile field even maybe like a forest of goodness for The Lord.

Proverbs: 14 verse 31   Feb 19

> He who oppresses the poor shows contempt
> for their Maker but whoever is kind
> to the needy honours
> God.

Who of us that belong to God would want to oppress the poor? However this does seem to happen

sometimes without us even knowing until it is pointed out to us by God. The poor are not only those without financial or worldly goods but are those poor souls without Jesus. The kindest thing we can do is to tell them about Him as well as befriending them.

John: 1 verse 12 — Feb 20

> But as many as received Him, to them gave He power to become the sons of God, even to them that believe on His name:

We must believe on the Name of Jesus if we want to be a Son of God. Are you a Son of God? If not how about inviting Jesus into your heart today, even this minute, so that you can be a Son of the most high God. It is something us as Christians treasure, having Jesus in our hearts.

Psalm: 1 verse 1 — Feb 21

> Blessed is the man that walketh not in the counsel of the ungodly.......

Today is a new day, let us not walk in or listen to the counsel of those who are ungodly, let us be guided by The Holy Spirit of Jesus and have a lovely day.

John: 1 verse 3   **Feb 22**

Through Him all things were made; without Him nothing was made that has been made. Look around today and see the wonder of God's

Creation. It is beautiful and so are you, God made you just as you are and He loves you.

Isaiah: 61 verse 3   **Feb 23**

……the garment of praise for the spirit of heaviness;

That is what God has given us, so if you feel a bit down at the moment begin to Praise Him, then the spirit of heaviness will begin to move off. Try it and see, put on Christian music or a Christian Video and you will truly find the heaviness lifts off.

Luke: 2 verses 6 - 8   **Feb 24**

Blessed by The Lord God of Israel.

Heavenly Father you are The Lord God of Israel, I bless your Holy Name and wait for the day that you send your Son Jesus back to Zion your Holy City.

Psalm: 10 verse 4 — Feb 25

In his pride the wicked does not seek Him; in
all his thoughts there is no room for God.

Let us try to make a bit more room in our hearts today for God. Our thoughts come from our hearts and out of our mouth the heart speaks. People will know if we have made room for God by the things we say, let our thoughts today be more holy.

John: 13 verse 3 — Feb 26

Jesus knew that the Father had put all things under His power and that He had come from God and was returning to God;

As Christians we have been given the Power that Jesus bestowed upon us to use for His Kingdom while we live on this earth, then when our time is right we shall return to God our maker in Heaven to be with Jesus. Let us make good use today of that divine power and walk in the love of The Lord Jesus.

Romans: 3 verse 23 — Feb 27

"For all have sinned and come
short of the glory of God"

It is sad that we have all sinned and come short of the glory of God but Jesus has forgiven our sins and we can press on today knowing that there is no condemnation in Christ Jesus. So don't be weighed down by sin. If you have committed a fresh sin, repent, ask Jesus to forgive you, thank Him and press on in faith and have a good day.

Psalm: 13 verse 6　　　　　　　　　　　Feb 28

> I will sing to The LORD, for He
> has been good to me.

The LORD loves to hear us sing, so what are we waiting for - Let us: Sing, sing, sing - today.

James: 1 verse 5　　　　　　　　　　　Feb 29

If any of you lacks wisdom, he should ask God, who gives generously to all without finding fault and it will be given to him.

I love wisdom, how about you? However naïve or unskilled we are, if we ask God for wisdom He gives it to us - the above verse says - generously. We can all be wise but we must remember to ask for wisdom, what a privilege to be able to ask and receive!

Share the PEACE
of The Lord

March

PRAYER

Dear God I pray that I may be filled with
Righteousness that comes through your
Son Jesus Christ (Philippians 1 v 11)
I pray that Jesus may be Lord of my life
for ever and ever.

May I grow in your love God and be
filled evermore with your Holy Spirit,
also with your fruits and gifts of the Holy Spirit.
That you may use me to help others.
I pray that I may be so filled with your love,
peace and joy that it may emanate through me
for others to see.

That they may come to know Jesus,
that He died for us on the cross.
I pray that my sins are forgiven,
- please God and help me to know when
you have forgiven me each time. - Please God,
so that I can feel that release in my Spirit
to do your will each day and for ever.

I pray that I never forget or take for granted
that Jesus died for my sins on the cross,
that only through Him am I saved.
Giving you my body for your Holy Spirit
to work through and use as a temple for you God.
May I ever know your saving grace
and live in your Kingdom forever.
Amen.

Psalm: 23 verse 3   Mar 1

> He restores my soul, He guides me in paths
> of righteousness for His mane's sake.

Thank you LORD that you restore my soul, so that I do not long for worldly things but can walk in righteousness to the best of the ability that you give me today.

James: 1 verses 2 - 3   Mar 2

Consider it pure joy, my brothers, whenever you face trials of many kinds, because you know that the testing of your faith develops perseverance.

We don't usually face trials with joy do we? If only we could use our faith more in the difficult circumstances, persevere in faith and let God be in charge instead of ourselves, we would find life much easier. Maybe you are in a difficult situation today, remember the disciples - we must have faith even as small as a mustard seed. Let us not give up in the testing of our faith, don't let the devil have the upper hand, especially today.

Psalm: 27 verse 1   Mar 3

> The Lord is my light and my Salvation
> - whom shall I fear?

Remember perfect love casts out all fear! Jesus loves us with a perfect love, let us love Him with that love, then we need have no fear!

Romans: 14 verse 17   Mar 4

For the Kingdom of God is not a matter of eating and drinking but of righteousness, peace and joy in the Holy Spirit.

Today let us walk with The Holy Spirit of Jesus in that lovely peace and joy that only comes from The Kingdom of God.

Psalm: 31 verse 5   Mar 5

Into your hands I commit my spirit; redeem me, O LORD, the God of truth.
We need to commit ourselves afresh each day to The LORD our God. Have you done that today?

1 Corinthians: 7 verses 2-3   Mar 6

But since there is so much immorality, each man should have his own wife and each woman her own husband. The husband should fulfil his marital duty to his wife and likewise the wife to her husband. The wife's body does not belong to her alone but also to her husband.

This is pretty awesome when you think about it and is quite profound, we really should take note and act in the way that we were made regarding husband and wife.

Luke: 3 verse 11 — Mar 7

John answered, "The man with two tunics should share with him who has none and the one who has food should do the same."

Is there anyone today that you can bless with a gift? It's lovely to be able to share. I don't mean an expensive gift. There maybe someone near you who is unemployed, disabled, sick or in need of even a nice loaf of bread, biscuits, cake, an item of clothing. The main thing is when you share, it is a gift of love. As Christians we can bring a lot of pleasure to those in need and it could be a chance to share the Gospel.

Jude: verse 21 — Mar 8

Keep yourselves in God's love as you wait for the mercy of our Lord Jesus Christ to bring you to eternal life.

What about today then, are we really keeping ourselves in God's love? Can we show that love of Jesus to someone today - just a small act of kindness, even a smile to someone will show God that we are waiting in His love.

Proverbs: 4 verse 1 — Mar 9

Listen, my sons, to a father's instruction; pay attention and gain understanding.

Yes please Heavenly Father, help me to listen to your instruction, so that I can receive more understanding today.

James: 1 verse 26 — Mar 10

If anyone considers himself religious and yet does not keep a tight reign on his tongue, he deceives himself and his religion is worthless.

Today let us be extra careful of the words we use, a good thought is to not use any derogatory words or negative words. We really must try hard to keep a tight reign on our tongue, if we use uplifting words it should make all the difference to those who come before us today. Especially those who need a kind word from someone.

Psalm: 25 verse 1 — Mar 11

To you, O LORD, I lift up my soul;

Can you really say - I lift up my soul to you O LORD. Have you ever read this Psalm, if not how about reading it now during your prayer time?

Romans: 6 verse 4 — Mar 12

"We were buried with Him through baptism"

Have you been baptized in water, it says in the Bible that we need to be born again of Water and of the Spirit. Please consider having your Water Baptism soon if you have not already had it. As we come up through the water we have come through the Cross of Jesus burial into our New Life. We are a new creature in Christ,

Born Again into the Kingdom of Light.

If you are not sure of this, talk to a Christian who truly has Jesus in their heart. i.e. One who is Spiritually Born Again.

Psalm: 5 verse 4 — Mar 13

> You are not a God who takes pleasure in evil, with you the wicked cannot dwell.

As Christians let us not take pleasure in any of the evil things in the world. If we continue to be wicked, we know that we cannot live in the Kingdom of God because He hates evil. God loves us but does not like any of our evil ways. So let us get rid of anything that is not pleasing to God if we can today.

Psalm: 61 verse 3 — Mar 14

> For you have been my refuge, a
> strong tower against the foe.

I praise you God that you are my refuge, that as long as I put my trust in you, you will fight for me against anyone or anything that comes against me. And in the Name Jesus I put my trust. Thank you that I can.

2 Corinthians: 7 verse 10 — Mar 15

Godly sorrow brings repentance that leads to salvation and leaves no regret but worldly sorrow brings death.

When we truly repent our hearts can sing because we know that we are forgiven, that we will definitely try not to offend God in the way that we used to.

Godly sorrow is good because although we can be sad about the circumstance that has arisen we are blessed so much when we take hold of the fact that Jesus has forgiven us and that our sin is blotted out from Our Father in Heaven. In worldly sorrow there can be no joy, in Godly sorrow Jesus rejoices that we repent and grants us peace in our hearts.

Psalm: 33 verse 1   Mar 16

> Sing joyfully to The LORD, you righteous;
> It is fitting for the upright to praise Him.

Let us sing to The LORD a new song, let us sing again today, make up a song to sing if you can't remember any words to songs, just make some up and sing. O the devil doesn't like us singing to God so make a joyful noise and sing, chase your blues away. (That's if you have any)!

James: 3 verse 18   Mar 17

Peacemakers who sow in peace raise a harvest of righteousness.

Are you a Peacemaker - just think of the harvest of righteousness that you can reap for The LORD. When you think about the everyday world what a lovely thing it is to try to minister peace in the midst of some

of the strife that goes on. Even today one word of greeting to someone in a peaceful loving way can make all the difference to their day. And to ours.

Psalm: 22 verse 22   Mar 18

> I will declare your name to my brothers;
> In the congregation I will praise you.

Shall we start to declare the name of The LORD to those who are not our Brothers and Sisters in Christ. Yes we should, because The Gospel is to be preached throughout the Earth before Jesus will come back. So if we do our bit I'm sure it will help. It is good to praise in the congregation but we need to show the world that we do praise God.

James: 1 verse 17 — Mar 19

Every good and perfect gift is from above and cometh down from The Father of lights, with whom is no variableness, neither shadow of turning.

Think of all the wonderful gifts that have been poured down to us from The Father of lights, our Father in Heaven. He gives so graciously to us, who often are not worthy to receive. He loves us so much that He loves to bless us with perfect gifts. I thank you Heavenly Father for all the marvellous gifts you have given me, my family, my health, my food, my shelter, my friends, my work - the list is unending like your goodness to me is never-ending. Thank you Heavenly Father. Amen.

Psalm: 8 verse 1 — Mar 20

> O LORD, our LORD, how majestic
> is your name in all the Earth!

Your Name is majestic in all the Earth God. No other name can ever match your Name and the Name of Jesus. Your Name Jesus is beautiful, the Name above all Names. May we praise your name God our Heavenly Father and the Name of Jesus with all that is within us today.

1Corinthians: 13 verse 1   Mar 21

> ....but if I have not love, I am only a
> resounding gong or a clanging cymbal.

Imagine being empty and sounding like a clanging cymbal, we do need to be filled with love, the kind of love that only Jesus can give us. To receive His love so that we can give it out to others we really must want the love of God Our Heavenly Father and of Jesus Christ His Son to be in our hearts. By The Holy Spirit we then can share the Love of the Lord.

Psalm: 29 verse 1   Mar 22

> Ascribe to The LORD, O mighty ones,
> ascribe to The LORD glory and strength.

We may not be mighty ones but we can give The LORD Glory by the things we say and do each day. Let us do something nice for The Lord Jesus Today through Him God will receive the Glory from us!

One thing we can do is to praise and thank Him for our Salvation and how blessed we are through Jesus.

Luke: 6 verse 32 — Mar 23

If you love those who love you, what credit is that to you? even sinners love those who love them!

That's true isn't it! But as Christians we are meant to love the unlovely, just as Jesus did - to help them, befriend them, most of all to show them the love of Jesus. Even in our own families there are relatives that we feel we cannot be with for long, we have to overcome that feeling and remember God made them and we are not only to tolerate them but to love them. It can be a bit of a problem that Scripture but remember we are to overcome and nothing is impossible with God. So we had better ask Him for His grace to help us. It's amazing what happens when we ask His help.

Psalm: 6 verse 4 — Mar 24

> Turn, O LORD and deliver me; save
> me because of your unfailing love.

Your love God is unfailing, please deliver me today from all those that come against me in thought, word or spirit. I thank you God for your wonderful protection of me day by day. Amen.

2 Peter: 3 verse 18 — Mar 25

"Grow in grace and in the knowledge of our LORD and Saviour Jesus Christ"

One of the best ways to grow in grace and knowledge of God is to read the Bible, getting things second hand is not a good idea and really doesn't get us very far. So....if you are not reading your Bible, today is a very good time to start.

However if you are reading your Bible daily, then I pray that you will continue to grow in the knowledge and grace of Our Lord and Saviour Jesus Christ.

Amen.

Psalm: 28 verse 6 — Mar 26

Praise be to The LORD, for He
has heard my cry for mercy.

I am so glad that The LORD always hears my cry, He has mercy on me day after day. Do you find that as well? Whenever we need His help He is there for us, I am so glad that I belong to God.

Revelation: 2 verse 10   Mar 27

"Be faithful until death and I will give you a crown of life:

How lovely to have a crown of Life - to live forever in Eternity with Jesus. Think for a moment or two about

being faithful, let us try today to be as faithful as we can be to the Gospel of Christ.

Psalm: 112 verse 1   Mar 28

Praise The LORD. Blessed is the man who fears The Lord, who finds great delight in His commands.

The LORD's commands should be precious to us . Each day we need to remember His commands, especially the ways we are to live our lives on this earth. How you may ask - well the first and greatest commandment is to Love God with all our heart and with all our soul and our neighbour as ourselves. What blessings we receive when we try to put this great commandment into action!

Romans: 5 verse 8   Mar 29

"While we were yet sinners, Christ died for us"

Do we ever realise just how bad the sin was that we were born into? I don't think we could ever imagine it but The Lord Jesus knew and He alone as able to rescue us....Praise The Lord! Help us not to fall back into any kind of sin today please God. Amen.

Psalm: 32 verse 2 — Mar 30

> Blessed is the man whose sin The LORD does not count against him and in whose spirit is no deceit.

Dear LORD please let it be that there shall be no deceit in my spirit, so that I may be blessed afresh today.

1 Timothy: 6 verse 5 — Mar 31

.....................................who have been robbed of the truth and who think that godliness is a means to financial gain.

This Scripture applies to those who love money, yes we do need money and we have to work to earn it but we must not make it a god in our lives. Because God supplies all our needs, we cannot think that we can pray - please God send me a fortune in money. Best to read the above Scripture to get a really good meaning of this for our lives today, then get on with our Godly living in the knowledge that God supplies all our needs, financial or otherwise.

***

April

We are all individuals, all different as people, just as snowflakes are different but are still snowflakes. God made everyone according to a pattern. So we are made, according to a pattern.

We are made in the image of God.

1 Timothy: 6 verse 6 — April 1

But godliness with contentment is great gain.

To be content is something wonderful, we are to be content in all circumstances but most times we are definitely not! What do you think is the reason why we are not content? Could it be that we are not walking in godliness? I think that maybe a lot to do with it. Whatever is going on in your life today try to be content with what you have, try not to yearn for things that cannot be. Let us praise The Lord for what we already have.

Psalm: 26 verse 2 — April 2

> Test me, O Lord and try me, examine
> my heart and my mind;

Have you ever asked The Lord to examine your heart and mind. It makes you wonder when He examines us what will He find? I think it best to try to have a look into our own hearts before we ever ask The Lord to take a look. Our minds are sometimes a minefield, full of things that they should not be full of. We best get rid of some of the awful things that seem to come into our hearts and minds before we ask God to examine them. Maybe best to start straight away! Let me see, have I let go of worry, anger? Oh dear seems a lot of rubbish in there that should not be there, how about you?

2 John: 1 verse 6 — April 3

And this is love: that we walk in obedience to His commands. As you have heard from the beginning, His command is that you walk in love.

Please would you help me to walk in love today Lord! Amen.

Psalm: 30 verse 2 — April 4

> O LORD my God, I called to you
> for help and you healed me.

Yes LORD I can truly say that I did call to you for help and yes you did heal me of an incurable disease in my lungs - Bronchiectasis in 1984 in Perth, Western Australia. I give you all the praise and glory God that I can witness that you sent Jesus your Son to earth as our Saviour and Healer, thank you, thank you.

So if you need help for healing, today is a good time to ask The LORD God if He will allow Jesus to heal you. I pray that when you ask you will receive in good measure what ever you are asking for. Amen.

Proverbs: 1 verse 7 — April 5

The fear of The LORD is the beginning of knowledge but fools despise wisdom and instruction.

I think I shall ask The LORD for more knowledge and wisdom today, I do not want to be a fool, I pray that I do have the fear of The LORD and I certainly do not despise wisdom and knowledge. For my part I know that I do love wisdom and knowledge, also I do know that I definitely need more! Thank you LORD God that you continue to fill me afresh each day also with the knowledge and love of Jesus.

Psalm:: 47 verse 2　　　　　　　　　　April 6

> How awesome is The LORD Most High,
>　　the great King overall the earth!

God is awesome. Imagine how beautiful He must be surrounded by angels and by glorious light. What a privilege to belong to Him. When we go home to heaven we shall see Him as He is!

James: 1 verses 3 - 4　　　　　　　　April 7

Because you know that the testing of your faith develops perseverance. Perseverance must finish its work so that you may be mature and complete, not lacking anything.

Reading this we can see that we need to persevere, what ever the task is before us we must press on, we must not give up. What ever work we have to do today or what ever trouble or concerns are with us we must persevere for Jesus sake, so that even today we can become that bit more mature in Christ.

Psalm: 48 verse 10 — April 8

Like your name, O God your praise
reaches to the ends of the earth;
your right hand is filled with righteousness.

Thank you that you are a righteous God, you are my God and I love you my Heavenly Father, please accept my praise from this part of the earth.

Psalm: 51 verse 7 — April 9

"Wash me and I shall be whiter then snow."

Only you O God can cleanse me and make me whiter than snow, continue to take out of me anything that is unclean day by day, hour by hour, minute by minute to enable me to be fit for your Kingdom and to do your work please. Amen.

2 Peter: 3 verse 18 — April 10

"Grow in grace and in the knowledge of our Lord and Saviour Jesus Christ."

Dear God we can only grow in grace if we ask you for grace and you kindly grant it to us so that we can grow in the knowledge of our Lord and Saviour Jesus Christ. So today LORD God I pray that you will grant me more of your beautiful grace, thank you that I may receive it now. Amen.

Psalm: 71 verse 5   April 11

> For You have been my hope, O Sovereign LORD, my confidence since my youth.

I am very fortunate that I have known The LORD since my youth, the confidence that God gives is incredible. If you do not know Him, today is a good day to begin to seek Our Father in Heaven. If you do already know God and Jesus Christ our Lord then you are truly blessed.

Psalm: 12 verse 6   April 12

> And the words of The Lord are flawless, like silver refined in a furnace of clay, purified seven times.

What about our words - could we say they are flawless? I think not, most of the time we are very careless with our words. Let us ask The Holy spirit to speak through us and help us to curb our tongue. So that we may be more purified in our speaking.

Proverbs: 1 verse 8 — April 13

Listen, my son, to your father's instruction and do not forsake your mother's teaching.

How much more do we need to listen to Our Father in Heaven, who teaches us through the Word. Are you going to read or have you already read any of Gods Word in your Bible today?

Psalm: 38 verse 9 — April 14

All my longings lie open before you, O LORD;
my sighing is not hidden from you.

Please hear the longings of my heart today God, let your Holy spirit comfort me, I will not hide my thoughts from you, you are my God who blesses me when I allow my heart to be revealed to you.

Matthew: 12 verse 12 — April 15

"How much more valuable is a man than a sheep! Therefore it is lawful to do good on the Sabbath"

Which ever day you choose for your Sabbath, remember that we can still bless our neighbours, heal the sick, spread the Gospel, fellowship with other Christians. No way do we have to sit home and do nothing. Praise The Lord Jesus for the healings that He did on His Sabbath days.

Psalm: 24 verse 1   April 16

> The earth is The LORD's and everything
> in it, the world and all who live in it;

It is incredible to think that we were made by the Ruler of the Universe, let us show our appreciation in being obedient to Him.

Malachi: 4 verse 4   April 17

Remember the law of my servant Moses, the decrees and laws I gave Him at Horeb for all Israel.

Do you remember the law that was given to Moses? We know that as Christians we live by grace now and not by law. However we do need to live according to the Commandments that were given to Moses. If we break one we may as well have broken the lot because in the eyes of God - sin is sin however large or small. I am thankful that we can ask Jesus to forgive us and that He does, especially as we go before God asking for all that we seem to ask Him for!

Genesis: 1 verse 1   April 18

In the beginning God created the Heavens and the Earth.

As God created the Heavens and Earth, we must know that He created us as Human Beings and that we did not evolve. He made us in the likeness of His only Son Jesus. Think for a moment, no one suggests that Jesus evolved from an ape so why should anyone think that we did? Praise God that we are made in His likeness and be glad.

Psalm: 37 verse 4   April 19

> Delight yourself in The Lord and
> He will give you the desires of your heart.

Let us do that today, delight ourselves in God our Heavenly Father, tell Him we love Him and really mean it. Don't let words be just words, let us mean them with our whole heart when we say we love Him. To love Him is to be obedient and walk in the ways of Jesus. We know that God already knows the desires of our hearts but it is good to let Him know that we do love Him for Himself - not just for what we get from Him.

Proverbs: 1 verse 10 — April 20

My son, if sinners entice you, do not give in to them.

If someone asks you to sin today please say no! It's as simple as that. The devil cannot make us do wrong things it is up to us to choose. So let us try today not to do those wrong things. In any case it will save us having to ask Jesus to forgive us again for that sin. That's worth thinking about!

Galatians: 1 verse 3 — April 21

Grace and peace to you from God our Father and the Lord Jesus Christ.

It is lovely today to know the grace and peace that can only come from God and Jesus. If you have a spare minute right now, sit and receive that wonderful peace, remember ask and you shall receive.

Psalm: 36 verse 9 — April 22

> For with you is the fountain of life;
> in your light we see light.

Yes LORD it is the Spiritual light that we see, the goodness that is in the world, everything of beauty has your life. Thank you for your divine light and life of our Holy spirit that dwells in us.

Acts: 8 verse 4 — April 23

Those who had been scattered preached the word wherever they went.

Today will be a good day for us to preach the word, even in a small way. If we tell someone about Jesus today it will help forward the Gospel of Peace.

Jude: 1 verses 17-18 — April 24

But dear friends, remember what the apostles of our Lord Jesus Christ foretold. They said to you, "in the last times there will be scoffers who will follow their own ungodly desires"

Today, maybe we can try to follow Godly desires a bit better, it may be difficult sometimes but I for one do not want to be a scoffer, nor do I want to do ungodly things. If you are a Christian you will be feeling the same way, God will bless us for trying, that we do know.

Exodus: 11 verse 9 — April 25

The LORD had said to Moses, "Pharaoh will refuse to listen to you - so that my wonders may be multiplied in Egypt."

Do you realize that even today The LORD is still performing His wonders. If you do not know what is going on in this day and age, please find a spirit filled Church and read some of the reports that are coming in from around the world. It is incredible what the LORD is doing. The same now as 2000 years ago, healing the sick, giving sight to the blind, bringing people out of darkness into His Kingdom of Light. The list goes on, remember He needs us and wants us to participate with The Holy Spirit to accomplish the same works that Jesus did on earth.

Psalm: 39 verse 6   April 26

> Man is a mere phantom as he goes to and
> fro: he bustles about but only in vain;
> he heaps up wealth, not knowing who will get it.

Instead of heaping up wealth and belongings, let us gladly help our brothers and sisters when they are in need. Don't wait until you die to leave your inheritance to your children, help them when they need help. As you bless others you will be even more blessed, remember you will never out give God. Every time you bless someone you will feel blessed and you will be blessed.

1 Corinthians: 12 verse 12   April 27

The body is a unit, though it is made up of many parts; and though all its parts are many, they form one body.

The Church body is made up of many parts, i.e. you and me and all other Christians. Although we are all different and have different tasks to do in the church (the same as the parts on our body have different parts to play), we make up one body - The Church.

As our body finds it difficult to work if one part is out of action, so the Church finds it cannot function to the fullest extent if we do not do our part in it!

Proverbs: 10 verse 19   April 28

When words are many, sin is not absent but he who holds his tongue is wise.

I believe this really means that we should not indulge in idle talk or gossip, so today we best try to restrain our tongue because sometimes it seems to have a life of its own and we have to bring it into submission. So let us be wise in our speaking today!

John: 15 verses 1-2 — April 29

"I am the true vine and my Father is the gardener. He cuts off every branch in me that bears no fruit, while every branch that does bear fruit He prunes so that it will be even more fruitful.......

Jesus said the above - and let us face it, it can be very painful being pruned. However it is worth it when we realize that we shall be even more fruitful for Our Father in Heaven by the works that we do for Him. Let us start some of the pruning of our worldly ways ourselves. Now where can we start on this today?

Psalm: 40 verse 1 — April 30

> I waited patiently for The LORD; He
> turned to me and heard my cry.

I pray LORD that I may always wait for you and that you will hear my cry, wherever I may be at any time here on this earth. I pray The LORD hears your cry today for what ever your needs may be, also that you may have peace in your heart today. Amen.

***

May

Let us rejoice in The Lord Today.

Psalm: 35 verse 27   May 1

> May those who delight in my vindication
> shout for joy and gladness; may they always
> say, "The LORD be exalted, who delights
> in the well-being of His servant"

What a lovely verse - let us delight ourselves in The LORD today, let us delight in the fact that He is concerned for our well-being.

Genesis: 5 verse 1   May 2

..........When God created man, He made him in the likeness of God.

How about the then? We are made in the likeness of God our Heavenly Father! Not like apes, monkeys, or any other creature but in the likeness of God.

Exodus: 7 verse 1   May 3

Then The LORD said to Moses, "See I have made you like God to Pharaoh and your brother Aaron will be your prophet."

Now that we live in the New Testament Times, God wants that all should prophesy. Not that we should all be prophets but that we should learn to speak out the word of God to others, whenever He gives us a new word to speak. Each day is a good day to try to listen to what God is saying to us, whether it be for ourselves or for the Church.

Proverbs: 10 verse 2 — May 4

Ill-gotten treasures are of no value but righteousness delivers from death.

That is true isn't it? If we have something that we have received wrongly, however much we treasure it we will still have that feeling of guilt i.e. that it is an ill-gotten thing. We really can't take anything that we know God does not want us to have. What a release in our spirit we feel when we give back or release those wrong treasures. Jesus forgives and we are back in righteousness delivered from the feeling of death and can rejoice in our righteousness. Praise The Lord!

Psalm: 57 verse 9 — May 5

> I will praise you, O LORD, among the nations;
> I will sing of you among the peoples.

How about a song today! You may not feel like singing but you could try a little song for The LORD. It is surprising what happens when we sing, gloom and despair have to start moving away. The devil doesn't like us singing to God. How about giving it a try. If you already feel happy in God you could sing an extra song of love to Him.

1 John: 2 verse 24   May 6

See that what you have heard from the beginning remains in you. If it does, you also will remain in the Son and in the Father.

This means that you will be abiding in Christ. We must remember what we learnt in the beginning when we first became Christians. Don't let it all go and be forgotten, think back what a wonder it has been at times and walk in the way Jesus would be walking here today, with perseverance in your heart.

Psalm: 93 verse 1   May 7

> The LORD reigns, He is robed in majesty;
> The LORD is robed in majesty
> and is armed with strength.

To see you in your majesty LORD would be wonderful, while we live on this earth we can only imagine your glory, with angels around you crying holy, holy, holy. Although you are mighty in majesty, you are our strength, those of us who belong to you through Jesus Christ our Lord, praise you LORD God in your beauty and majesty.

1 Thessalonians: 5 verse 23 — May 8

May God himself, The God of peace, sanctify you through and through. May your whole spirit, soul and body be kept blameless at the coming of our Lord Jesus Christ.

Only God our Father in Heaven is able to do this as we submit ourselves to Him. Let us submit ourselves afresh each day to Him and receive His wonderful blessings.

Proverbs:16 verse 7 — May 9

When a man's ways are pleasing to The LORD, He makes even his enemies live at peace with Him.

So when our ways are pleasing to The LORD God, its good that He makes our enemies live at peace with us. Even though they do not like us or want to live or work with us for The LORD, He makes them live peaceably with us. As long as we are walking in righteousness we have divine protection.

Psalm: 41 verse 13 — May 10

Praise be to The LORD, the God of Israel, from everlasting to everlasting. Amen and Amen.

Our God is the God of Israel, we are part of His chosen people when we become born again into His Kingdom, we are His from everlasting to everlasting, through all eternity.

1 Samuel: 1 verse 18   Mar 11

She said, "May your servant find favour in your eyes.?" Then she went her way and ate something and her face was no longer downcast.

Today, let us too find favour in Our Father God's eyes, let us think of something nice to do for Him today. Then we too can celebrate with some thing good to eat and our face need not be downcast.

Isaiah: 61 verse 3   May 12

.....the garment of praise for the spirit of heaviness;

Do we have on a garment of heaviness today - well if we have, we best start praising The Lord. In the praises and in the singing the spirit of heaviness begins to lift off. It is up to us to remove the heaviness as fast as we can and not to sit and wallow in our misery. Yes I know that sometimes we have down days but remember as soon as we are able to begin to praise God for His mercies we will begin to feel better.

Revelation: 22 verse 7 May 13

"Behold, I am coming soon! Blessed is he who keeps the words of the prophecy in this book."

Yes, Jesus is coming soon, the above words are in the Holy Bible. Are we ready, are we waiting, are we hoping that Jesus is coming soon. What a blessing it will be when He does come. No one knows the hour or the day but He is coming and it maybe sooner than we think. Let us try to wait for Him in righteousness and truth.

Song of Songs: 2 verse 16 May 14

My lover is mine and I am His.........

Do you know that Jesus is the lover of our souls, He loves us so much that He died on The Cross for us. Do you know that I am His. Are you His own, do you belong to Jesus, have you asked Him to come into your heart. If so you belong to the beloved as well. Praise The Lord!

1 Timothy: 6 verse 6 May 15

But godliness with contentment is great gain.

Being filled with the love of God and being content is a wonderful feeling. Today let us try to be content just where we are, then we shall begin to be more godly I am sure.

Psalm: 63 verse 3 — May 16

> Because your love is better than
> life, my lips will glorify you.

Yesterday we talked about being filled with your love God and being content just where we are. Because of your love we can glorify you, your love is better than life, to feel your love enveloping us is so special, thank you for your eternal love.

Jude: 1 verse 21 — May 17

Keep yourselves in God's love as you wait for the mercy of our Lord Jesus Christ to bring you to eternal life.

Today we are talking about love again, yes please God help me to stay in your love while I wait for Jesus to come for me.

Mark: 1 verse 3 — May 18

"a voice of one calling in the desert, Prepare the way for The Lord, make straight paths for Him."

Let us today prepare the way for Jesus to come back by being obedient to Our Father in Heaven, wanting to do His will not our own.

Psalm: 150 verse 6 — May 19

> Let everything that has breath praise
> The LORD. Praise The LORD.

Yes LORD, we have your breath in us. As Christians, please help us with the love of Jesus and the anointing of The Holy Spirit to praise you more today.

Genesis: 1 verse 3 — May 20

And God said, "Let there be light" and there was light.

We praise you God for the light, so that we can see your wonderful creation. Thank you for the beauty of your Kingdom around us, the flowers, the trees, the creatures, the people that we shall be meeting today.

Proverbs: 18 verse 15 — May 21

The heart of the discerning acquires knowledge; the ears of the wise seek it out

Dear God I pray today that we may have a more discerning heart, a heart that yearns for knowledge of you

God . Let our ears listen to your voice and may we be wiser today than yesterday to seek your ways.

Amen.

Psalm: 64 verse 10 — May 22

Let the righteous rejoice in The LORD and take refuge in Him; let all the upright in heart praise Him!

Are we more righteous today than we were yesterday? I like to think that we maybe. However hard it is for us in our everyday living we must still try to be righteous for The LORD our God.

Proverbs: 20 verse 22 — May 23

Do not say, "I'll pay you back for this wrong!" Wait for The Lord and He will deliver you.

To often we want to get back at those who hurt us, yes we all fall into that trap at times. However, we must learn to forgive them for coming against us. It's surprising what The Lord will do then to deliver us from these hurts. Let us not want to pay any one back today for the wrong they have done to us whether it was intentional or unintentional!

Matthew: 6 verses 17-18　　　　　　　May 24

But when you fast, put oil on your head and wash your face, so that it will not be obvious to men that you are fasting but only to your Father, who is unseen; and your Father, who sees what is done in secret, will reward you.

We do need to be discreet about our fasting. It's no good going around telling people - I'm fasting for this or that, because we do not reap much reward that way. Be your normal self and fast in private for The Lord's will to be done in whatever you are praying for. Yes, He will reward you openly, even then you cannot boast that you did it! Praise Him for the answered prayer.

Matthew: 5 verse 27　　　　　　　　May 25

You have heard that is was said, 'Do not commit adultery'………

Do you know that you can commit adultery by just looking lustfully with your eyes. It's best to read the whole Scripture to understand that if we look lustfully, then in God's eyes we may have already committed adultery in our hearts. We must learn to look away from all wrong things.

Psalm: 60 verse 12   **May 26**

> With God we shall gain the victory and
> He will trample down our enemies.
> Thank you God that you truly will. Amen.

1 Samuel: 14 verse 36   **May 27**

............But the priest said, "Let us inquire of God here"

Today is a good day for us to inquire of God what He wants us to do. Let us ask in prayer, then let us not rush off to make a Cuppa or something else trivial, let us wait a few moments for Him to reply. Then thank Him, ask for His guidance to do whatever you believe He is saying to you at that time.

2 Corinthians: 12 verse 9   **May 28**

But He said to me, "My grace is sufficient for you, for my power is made perfect in weakness"

Remember that God's grace is sufficient, we may be weak in our body, soul, mind, heart, spirit - whatever but God's grace is sufficient in all circumstances as long as we trust Him and know Jesus as Lord in our lives.

Psalm: 62 verse 1 — May 29

> My soul finds rest in God alone; my
> salvation comes from Him.

When I sit and pray, do you know, my soul does find rest in God, I pray that you find rest in God today. We do know that our salvation comes from Him. God does love our souls to be at rest in Him whether we are at work, play or in prayer, So today let us be at rest in God as we get on with our daily tasks etc.,

Galatians: 1 verse 10 — May 30

Am I now trying to win the approval of men, or of God? Or am I trying to please men? If I were still trying to please men, I would not be a servant of Christ.

I praise The Lord Jesus that I serve Him and Our Father in Heaven - how about you? Things to so much better when we please God first. You have probably already found that to be true.

Proverbs: 9 verse 10 — May 31

"The fear of The LORD is the beginning of wisdom and knowledge of The Holy One is understanding."

The book of Proverbs is a marvellous book to help us with our every day living. The above verse is great, it doesn't mean to be frightened of The LORD but rather to fear doing wrong in His sight. We need to use wisdom and knowledge in our understanding to do what is right and proper in the sight of The Holy One - Our LORD God Almighty who reigns forever and ever. Amen.

> It is a fearful thing
> to fall
> into the Hands of the Living God.

June

The LORD IS MY Shepherd
is He
Your Shepherd?

Ephesians: 6 verse 11   June 1

Put on the full armour of God so that you can take your stand against the devil's schemes.

We certainly need the full armour of God on, because we are really lost with out it when the devil tries to come against us. if you are not sure about the armour please read the whole chapter to be completely ready as a sol- dier, in the Army of Christ.

Ephesians: 6 verse 14   June 2

Stand firm then, with the belt of truth buckled around your waist, with the breastplate of righteousness in place.

Are we standing firm today the, have we got the belt of truth buckled around our waist - oh! I do hope so. We should also have the breastplate of righteousness on. Who can stand against us when we walk in truth and righteousness. What a blessing we can be to others when we are walking righteously along the narrow path with The Lord Jesus.

Ephesians: 6 verse 15   June 3

and with your feet fitted with the readiness that comes from the gospel of peace.

The gospel of peace is the Word of God. The feet that take the gospel to others are surely blessed by God. Our feet must be ready to go to who-ever and to where-ever The Lord wants us to go today.

Ephesians: 6 verse 16 — June 4

In addition to all this, take up the shield of faith, with which you can extinguish all the flaming arrows of the evil one.

Do you know that some of the flaming arrows, are the awful thoughts that the devil puts into our minds. We need faith to get rid of those thoughts, tell them to go, then praise The Lord. Praise exercise your faith. Practice your faith in the Word as you use your shield today. Then you will have victory over all the flaming arrows, even those that come from people we know and meet each day.

Ephesians: 6 verse 17 — June 5

Take the helmet of salvation and the sword of the Spirit, which is the Word of God.

Our head is protected by salvation, that is our helmet as a soldier of Christ. Our sword is so sharp it is the Word of God. Let us use it when-ever we can, the devil doesn't like us using the sword, his demons have to scatter away from us. Praise The Lord.

Ephesians: 6 verse 18 — June 6

And pray in the Spirit on all occasions with all kinds of prayers and requests. With this in mind, be alert and always keep on praying for all the saints.

Pray in the Spirit, The Holy Spirit of Jesus. Ask Him to help you pray and He will. God loves us to pray, it is our way of talking to Him. We need to know Jesus in our hearts before our prayers can be accomplished by Our Heavenly Father through The Holy Spirit. Yes we do need to pray for each other, all of us need help, none of us are clever enough to go through life on this earth without the Love of God and the prayers of the saints.

Ephesians: 6 verses 19-20 — June 7

Pray also for me, that whenever I open my mouth, words may be given me so that I will fearlessly make known the mystery of the gospel, for which I am an ambassador in chains. Pray that I may declare it fearlessly, as I should.

It was Paul who said the above, however I believe it applies to all of us who walk with Jesus and want to declare the Gospel Sometimes we feel that we are not free to declare the gospel but we are free and must ask that The Lord make the way for us to speak out to those souls around us who are in darkness who do not know Jesus. Let us pray that when we open our mouths that the right words also be given to us today.

Psalm: 54 verse 2   June 8

> Hear my prayer, O God; listen to
> the words of my mouth.

Yesterday we asked that the right words be given to us to speak to others about Jesus. Today when we ask God to listen to the words of our mouth, let us hope and pray that they are righteous words. So that He will hear our prayers, then we shall surely be blessed today.

1 Thessalonians: 5 verse 12   June 9

Now we ask you, brothers, to respect those who work hard among you, who are over you in The Lord and who admonish you.

Those who are over us in The Lord are our Priests, Ministers, our Pastors etc., we must show them respect today and every day. Also we need to pray for them, that they will faithfully minister the Word of The Lord in truth to us. That they continue in good health and that they receive protection from God for themselves and their families.

Proverbs: 10 verse 8 — June 10

The wise in heart accepts commands but a chattering fool comes to ruin.

Oh! God let us not be chattering fools today, let us try to be wise in our hearts and our speaking. Amen.

2 Thessalonians: 1 verse 11 — June 11

With this in mind, we constantly pray for you, that our God may count you worthy of His calling and that by His power He may fulfil every good purpose of yours and every act prompted by your faith.

I pray today that you will feel worthy to be called by God and will know what He wants you to do for Him today. As you walk in your faith you will see things being fulfilled that you have been asking and seeking God for. Know that God sees you as worthy, because He has called you and you will know this if your have truly accepted Jesus as your Lord and Saviour.

Psalm: 55 verse 22 — June 12

Cast your cares on The LORD and He will sustain you; He will never let the righteous fall.

Isn't that marvellous, that our God will sustain us! Whatever our circumstance, being righteous in Jesus Christ when we call on God He does hear us.

John: 4 verses 13-14 — June 13

Jesus answered, "Everyone who drinks this water will be thirsty again but whoever drinks the water I give him will never thirst. Indeed, the water I give him will become in him a spring of water welling up to eternal life"

What is this water that Jesus gives us that wells up in us like a spring? I believe that it is the infilling of The Holy Spirit that fills us and prepares us for eternal life. Today let us ask God for a new drink of His Holy Spirit in our hearts and lives, that we shall be refreshed and work today for Jesus, preparing ourselves for eternal life!

Mark: 13 verse 31 — June 14

Heaven and earth will pass away but my words will never pass away.

Jesus said the above words and it is true isn't it, when you think about it, it is now over 2000 years and the words of Jesus are still relevant today.

Proverbs: 28 verse 6   June 15

Better a poor man whose walk is blameless than a rich man whose ways are perverse.

Today let us try to walk a blameless life whether we are rich or poor financially. To be blameless is to have a clean heart and hands, to walk in God's ways.

Genesis: 1 verse 27   June 16

So God created man in His own image, in the image of God he created him; male and female He created them.

We have been created in God's image, just as Jesus walked on earth in the image of God, so are we made. Not as evolutionists advocate that we come from apes. Praise The Lord we are male and female according to His will.

Genesis: 9 verse 4   June 17

But you must not eat meat that has it's life blood still in it.

These are the words that God gave to Noah and that message is still there for us today. God wants that we should eat meat and all green plants that He has given us for food. The animal must first be killed before it becomes our meat.

Psalm: 56 verse 12 — June 18

> I am under vows to you, O God;
> I will present my thank-offerings to you.

I want to offer you something today LORD but I am not sure what to give. Being under vows to you God I present myself. One thing I can give - as a thank-offering is my praise. Yes I praise you today and thank you LORD for all your blessings to me. Amen.

Isaiah: 48 verse 10 — June 19

See, I have refined you, though not as silver; I have tested you in the furnace of affliction.

Do you sometimes feel that you are going through some dreadful affliction - well praise The Lord because through it He is refining you. We cannot always see the things He is doing in our lives by way of afflictions until we are able to look back after the event and can see the refining that has been done in the affliction. We must trust in God.

Matthew: 11 verse 12 — June 20

"How much more valuable is a man than a sheep! Therefore it is lawful to do good on the Sabbath"

Jesus said the above words. Have you read what this is all about in the above chapter. On the Sabbath, the day we choose for our day of rest, we are still to help anyone who comes to us for help. Jesus healed on the Sabbath, that was what all the fuss was about. Praise The Lord that we are more enlightened than the Pharisees were.

Psalm: 52 verse 9   June 21

I will praise you forever for what you have done; in your name I will hope, for your name is good. I will praise you in the presence of your saints.

In the presence of your saints God, that is - my fellow Christians, yes I will praise You, for everything that You have done and are doing for me through Jesus Christ my Lord and Saviour. My hope is in you forever and ever. Amen.

Proverbs: 6 verse 9   June 22

How long will you lie there, you sluggard? When will you get up from your sleep?

O LORD help me not to be lazy in your Kingdom, wake up my spirit each day, even today that I may not be classed as a sluggard i.e. a lazy person. Fill me today with an eagerness to do your will and please enable me to do it! Amen.

Hebrews: 13 verse 2 — June 23

Do not forget to entertain strangers, for by so doing some people have entertained angels without knowing it.

How wonderful to know that we may have talked to angels and looked after angels without knowing it. When we get to Heaven these things may be revealed to us - what a surprise it will be if we have. Let us show hospitality to those who come before us each day, even those who just pop in for a Cuppa. As you fellowship together over a cup of tea etc., it's amazing what God can do.

1 Corinthians: 1 verse 10 — June 24

I appeal to you, brothers, in the name of our Lord Jesus Christ, that all of you agree with one another so that there may be no divisions among you and that you may be perfectly united in mind and thought.

Today let us try to be united with our fellow Christians, especially in our local Church, so that our fellowship times each week when we come together as part of the family of Christ will be blessed even more by God.

Zechariah: 8 verse 17   June 25

Do not plot evil against your neighbour and do not love to swear falsely. I hate all this, declares The LORD.

When we look at the above Scripture, we can clearly see that The LORD has feelings. Today let us not hurt His feelings by thinking or doing wrong things or by speaking untruthfully. As Christians we know all theses things but it becomes a different matter when we try to put them into practice, especially having bad thoughts about our neighbours sometimes. Help! Bless me today LORD with beautiful thoughts.

Amen.

Psalm: 74 verse 16   June 26

> The day is Yours and Yours also the night;
> You established the sun and moon.

Thank you LORD that the day is Yours, even today as we live, this is your day. Thank You for today that I may walk in the Love of Jesus and fellowship with your lovely Holy Spirit.

Acts: 20 verse 10   **June 27**

Paul went down, threw himself on the young man and put his arms around him. "Don't be alarmed," he said "He's alive!"

Praise The Lord that we are alive. May6be today would be a good day to wrap our arms around some one, to tell them that we love them with the love of The Lord Jesus. What a lovely thing to do.

Proverbs: 18 verse 16   **June 28**

A gift opens the way for the giver and ushers him into the presence of the great.

A gift we can give, to come into the presence of God, is our praise. When we go to visit someone in the world, a gift however small, given with love opens the door, as a way to communicate. It can even open the way to share the Gospel to unbelievers.

Matthew: 11 verse 28   **June 29**

Come to me, all you who are weary and burdened and I will give you rest.

Now are we feeling burdened or weary today? Right, well if we are let us give all those burdens to The Lord and we know that when we really hand them over He does give us rest. However large or small, if we put them into His charge we can rest in His peace. So right now Lord Jesus I give you all my worries and burdens and receive your wonderful peace. Thank you Lord. Amen.

Matthew: 11 verse 29   June 30

Take my yoke upon you and learn from me, for I am gentle and humble in heart and you will find rest for your souls.

The rest we spoke of yesterday is marvelous when we have given over our burdens to The Lord. But just think, when we take up His Yoke it is not a burden, because He gives us rest in our souls! When our souls are at rest in Jesus, in God our Father, what a beautiful place to be. I pray that you find rest in your soul today as you work for our Saviour Jesus Christ our Lord. Amen.

Allelujah - Praise The Lord.

July

> Let us submit ourselves
> afresh today.
> To Our Father in Heaven.
> Let us walk in the Love of Jesus
> and
> in Fellowship with The Holy Spirit.

Psalm: 19 verse 1 — July 1

> The heavens declare the Glory of God; the
> skies proclaim the work of His hands.

Yes LORD the heavens do declare your Glory and in the skies we can see the work of your hands. Today let us declare the work of God, the wonders that God has already done in our lives, let us say to our friends and neighbours Praise The LORD.!

John: 4 verse 22 — July 2

Samaritans worship what you do not know; we worship what we do know, for salvation is from the Jews.

Jesus said the above and it is true, so we do need to pray for the Jews and thank God for His grace that He receives us Gentiles into Salvation. Let us be thankful today for incredible love of Our Father in Heaven.

1 Corinthians: 6 verse 1 — July 3

If any of you has a dispute with another dare he take it before the ungodly for judgement in stead of before the saints?

In other words if you have an argument or dispute why not sort it out in Church in the presence of God and ask Jesus to resolve the problem between you instead of running to someone who is not a Christian? Today if problems arise let us show the love of Jesus.

Ester: 3 verse 5 — July 4

When Haman saw that Mordecai would not kneel down or pay Him honour, he was enraged.

We as Christians cannot pay honour to anything of Satan. Yes, people will be enraged at our attitude but we best stick with Jesus so that we do not anger The LORD God Almighty. We best fear The LORD not the devil so that we have divine protection from all wrong things today and forever. Amen.

Proverbs: 1 verse 10 — July 5

My son, if sinners entice you, do not give in to them.

This much the same message as yesterday, so can we say today we shall not sin! Thank you Lord Jesus that you will help me please by your Holy Spirit not to fall into sin today. Amen.

Psalm: 34 verse 18 — July 6

> The LORD is close to the broken-hearted
> and saves those who are crushed in spirit.

We all get broken hearted and crushed in our spirit at sometime during our lives here on this earth. Let us remember to come to God at those times, sit at His feet, give Him our burdens and He will comfort us by His Holy spirit, whom Jesus sent to be our comforter. Today if this is a day of any sort of burden for you, please know that God is very close to you.

Luke: 9 verse 62 — July 7

Jesus replied, "No one who puts his hand to the plow and looks back is fit for service in the Kingdom of God"

Let us stop looking back today to what might have been. Let us look forward with a vision of what the Lord Jesus wants us to do for The Kingdom. Whatever it is, large or small, let us do it with love, with the grace of God and a cheerful heart. How pleased Our Father will be when we say we did it Lord and how much happier our day will be.

John: 11 verse 27 — July 8

"Yes, Lord," she told him "I believe that you are the Christ, the Son of God, who was to come into the world."

Martha, said the above words when she was talking to Jesus. Have you read the above chapter, it tells us such a lot about Martha and Mary. Do you truly believe that Jesus is the Christ, the Son of God? I do hope so. If you are not a Christian, I pray that you soon will be able to invite Jesus into your heart and become one. Amen.

Luke: 2 verse 19 — July 9

But Mary treasured up all these things and pondered them in her heart.

Sometimes it is good for us to treasure things in our heart. Let us not treasure things that God would not want us to hold on to. Let us treasure the things of The Kingdom of God, so that our soul may be at peace with God. Remember, we need no earthly treasure.

Psalm: 21 verse 13 — July 10

> Be exalted, O Lord, in your strength; we
> will sing and praise your might.

We will sing and praise your might LORD God. We shall sing, so that you may be exalted on high for ever and ever. Today also we acknowledge your great strength in all things. Fill us today with your wonderful joy LORD, enable us to praise you more each day.

Luke: 4 verses 18-19　　　　　　　　July 11

"The Spirit of The Lord is on me, because He has anointed me to preach good news to the poor. He has sent me to proclaim freedom for the prisoners and recovery of sight for the blind, to release the oppressed, to proclaim the year of The Lord's favour."

Today we can proclaim the Gospel of the Lord Jesus Christ. Praise Him that He will anoint us to do so. Let us ask for His special anointing of The Holy spirit afresh today.

John: 14 verses 16-17　　　　　　　　July 12

And I will ask The Father and He will give you another Counsellor to be with you forever - The Spirit of truth. The world cannot accept Him because it neither sees Him nor knows Him. But you know Him, for He lives with you and will be in you.

Isn't that marvellous, that we can know the wonderful Holy spirit, who will comfort us today and forever when we ask Him to.

Psalm: 20 verse 1　　　　　　　　July 13

May The LORD answer you when you are in distress; may the name of the God of Jacob protect you.

If the LORD God is your God have no doubt that He will protect you in all circumstances today and forever. Praise The LORD that He really does.

Luke: 18 verse16 — July 14

But Jesus called the children to Him and said, "Let the little children come to me; and do not hinder them, for the Kingdom of God belongs to such as these."

Today are we helping the little children to know Jesus, we must know Him ourselves before we can bring the children to Him. I pray that we know Jesus more and more each day, especially today. Amen.

Hebrews: 13 verse 1 — July 15

Keep on loving each other as brothers.

Today let us keep that commandment of God to love... our brothers as ourselves. How much more peaceful our day will be when we have no malice or hate in our hearts toward our brothers, just the love of The Lord toward them.

Proverbs: 29 verse7 — July 16

The righteous care about justice for the poor but the wicked have no such concern.

Praise The Lord that He allows us to be righteous as Christians so that we do care about justice for the poor. Today let us pray for those who are poor, not only financially but especially for those who are poor in spirit, those that do not know our Lord Jesus.

John: 6 verse 26 — July 17

"Do not work for food that spoils but for food that endures to eternal life, which the Son of Man will give you. On Him God The Father has placed His seal of approval"

The above was said by Jesus and how true it is that we should seek the food of the Word of God and not food that spoils. Today let us seek out more truth of the Gospel for our own sake, for our eternal life.

Psalm: 53 verse 2 — July 18

God looks down from Heaven on the sons of men to see if there are any who understand, any who seek God.

Are we seeking God today, are we asking His help today. Do we care about God today? Are we trusting in God for all our needs today? He is looking to see!

Matthew: 24 verse 42   July 19

Therefore keep watch, because you do not know on what day your Lord will come.

How do we keep watch? Well I believe that to keep watch is to try to be ready, to have our house in order, that is to say have our hearts prepared, ready and waiting, just incase it is today - that Jesus comes.

Matthew: 24 verse 44   July 20

So you also must be ready because The Son of Man will come at an hour when you do not expect him.

So you also must be ready, that means me as well, each of us must try, like we said yesterday to get our houses, our hearts, cleaned up, all the gunk and junk out, ready for when He comes. Let us let go of bitterness, strife, hate and jealousy, lies, covetousness, the list gone and on, lets get rid of them and Praise The Lord.

Psalm: 50 verse 1   July 21

The Mighty One, God, The LORD,
speaks and summons the earth
from the rising of the sun to the place where it sets.

Imagine, The LORD almighty has chosen you and me because He loves us. He also speaks to you and me and summons us, even as He speaks and summons the earth and all that is in it. Let us thank Him today that He is in charge of us, even as He is in charge of Eternity.

Ecclesiastes: 1 verse 3   July 22

What does man gain from all his labour at which he toils under the sun?

Well what shall we gain today if we labour and toil? Not much if we do not pray and rest in The Lord. Remember, His burden is light. He does not want us to wear ourselves out. Let us ask Him what work He wants us to do today. Make room today to sit and rest in The Lord, even if only for a few minutes to be refreshed in your spirit and soul.

Proverbs: 26 verse 2   July 23

Like a fluttering sparrow or a darting swallow, an underserved curse does not come to rest.

If we are walking in the light, in the light of The Lord, in righteousness and trust, then the curses that come from others lips cannot come to rest on us. Praise The Lord for His wonderful protection today. Amen.

1 Corinthians: 15 verse 58   July 24

Therefore, my dear brothers, stand firm. Let nothing move you. Always give yourselves fully to the work of the Lord, because you know that your labour in the Lord is not in vain.

Our labour in The Lord is definitely not in vain, He sees all the things that we do for Him. Everything is recorded of our works. So today maybe we could do something nice for The Lord Jesus.

1 Corinthians: 15 verses 51-52   July 25

Listen, I tell you a mystery: We will not all sleep but we will all be changed - in a flash, in the twinkling of an eye, at the last trumpet. For the trumpet will sound, the dead will be raised imperishable and we will be changed.

We will be changed, Praise The Lord, with immortality, we shall have imperishable bodies just like Jesus our Lord. Maybe not today but one day - maybe soon!

Psalm: 49 verse 20   July 26

> A man who has riches without understanding
> is like the beasts that perish.

O LORD, today grant us more understanding, knowledge and wisdom so that we can use the riches that you allow us to have, to further your kingdom on this earth. Amen.

1 Corinthians: 16 verse 9   July 27

Because a great door for effective work has opened to me and there are many who oppose me.

That often happens doesn't it? We see an opening for us to do something nice for The Lord and people come and oppose us! Well it is time we did not listen to those who come against us and continue in the work that The Lord has given us! Today is a good day to begin.

Acts: 17 verse 24   July 28

The God who made the world and everything in it is The LORD of Heaven and earth and does not live in temples built by hands.

There can be the most beautiful church buildings that we can go into to worship God but He does not live in them. He is Spirit and He allows His Spirit to live in us. Our bodies are temples that are made by Him for His Spirit to reside in. When we ourselves are born again into His Kingdom by accepting Jesus God's Son into our hearts He comes and dwells in us by His Spirit. Just think even today we are temples of the living God.

Proverbs: 25 verse 21 — July 29

If your enemy is hungry, give him food to eat; if he is thirsty, give him water to drink.

Today when people come against us in any way, we must remember to be charitable to them! Then The Lord will bless us. Our enemy should be blessed by us.

Proverbs: 27 verse 9 — July 30

Perfume and Incense bring joy to the heart and the pleasantness of one's friend springs from his earnest counsel.

It does bring joy to our heart when we can earnestly seek our friend who shows consideration toward us. It may be good to listen to his advise today.

Psalm: 51 verse 10 — July 31

Create in me a pure heart, O God and renew a steadfast spirit within me..

Yes please would you continue to do that for me today God. Let my spirit be steadfast for Jesus and help me to purify my heart for you. Amen.

Today is a good day
to
Praise The Lord.

August

Psalm: 58 verse 11 — Aug 1

Then men will say, "Surely the righteous still are rewarded; surely there is a God who judges the earth"

Because God says that we shall be rewarded, then we know that He will reward us for sure. However, we do need to be righteous, we cannot expect rewards for nothing. God blesses us with all good things. How He will surely reward us when we become even more righteous. I think we ought to make a special effort today to live a good life because God is our judge, who gives according to His will.

Genesis: 1 verse 5 — Aug 2

God called light "day" and the darkness He called "night". And there was evening and there was morning—the first day.

The night was dark and the day was light, for all these years since God made them they have been called the same - night and day. God does not chop and change things as we do, His word stands forever. Today, let us walk in His light.

Genesis: 1 verse 8 — Aug 3

God called the expanse "sky". And there was evening and there was morning - the second day.

Evening is surely then the beginning of the new day? How about that; it makes you think that we may have a few things the wrong way around. Maybe we better study the Word a bit more today?

Proverbs: 28 verse 9 Aug 4

If anyone turns a deaf ear to the law, even his prayers are detestable.

Today we best not turn a deaf ear to the law of the land. Even though as Christians we come under a different covenant we must still acknowledge and abide by the laws that govern our Country. Have a good day, living at peace with your neighbour today.

John: 4 verse 29 Aug 5

"Come, see a man who told me everything I ever did. Could this be the Christ?"

That was the woman at the well talking - how true it is for us as well, that Jesus knows everything that we have ever done in our lives. Today maybe we should think more carefully before we do some things? I know I had better think more carefully, how about yourself?

Psalm: 59 verse 16 — Aug 6

> But I will sing of your strength, in the morning. I will sing of your love; for you are my fortress, my refuge in times of trouble.

Today I will sing, I will sing unto The LORD because God your love toward me is very great. Thank you LORD God.

Revelation: 22 verse 6 — Aug 7

The angel said to me, "These words are trustworthy and true. The LORD, the God of the spirits of the prophets, sent His angel to show His servants the things that must soon take place."

Do you know that even today God speaks through His prophets here on this earth the things that are going to take place before they happen! Praise God that He also speaks by His Holy Spirit to us. If you have never heard God speak to you, sit quietly in your prayer time and ask Him to. Just wait awhile then in the quietness of your heart He will speak. Know that He loves you and wants that you should hear His voice.

Jude: 1 verse 20 — Aug 8

But you, dear friends, build yourselves up in your most holy faith and pray in The Holy Spirit.

O Lord Jesus we cannot do anything of ourselves, we need your blessed Holy Spirit to help us to pray. Holy Spirit I am so glad that Jesus sent you to be with us, to help us and comfort us, thank you that you do help us to pray.

1 John: 5 verse 1   Aug 9

Everyone who believes that Jesus is the Christ is born of God and everyone who loves The Father loves His Child as well.

Yes I do love you Jesus. Amen.

2 John: verse 4   Aug 10

It has given me great joy to find some of your children walking in the truth, just as The Father commanded us.

If St. John were here today he would find great joy in seeing us walk in the truth of The Lord Jesus. Today let us truly live as Our Father commanded us, as we do, we shall feel so blessed.

3 John: verse 14   Aug 11

I hope to see you soon and we will talk face to face.

John said the above while writing to his friends and I was just thinking it would be lovely to talk face to face with you. It is lovely when we as Christians can talk to each other about the love of Jesus isn't it? As I can't see you today to talk to I would like to say that I hope you have a lovely day. God Bless you.

2 Peter: 1 verse 3   Aug 12

His divine power has given us everything we need for life and godliness through our knowledge of Him who called us by his own glory and goodness.

Has Jesus called you, yes I believer He has. So today is a good day to thank Him, for not only calling your but for the calling that He has given your regarding the work that He wants you to do for The Kingdom.

Praise The Lord!

Psalm: 83 verse 18   Aug 13

Let them know that you, whose name is The LORD - that You alone are the Most High over all the earth.

Yes LORD God we acknowledge that you alone are the most High God. You are our God our Father in Heaven, Almighty God the Ancient of Days.

1 Peter: 5 verse 6   Aug 14

Humble yourselves, therefore, under God's mighty hand, that He may lift you up in due time.

Do you realise that when we do humble ourselves, to God, He does lift us up out of what ever situation we are in. If only we would remember and pray more humbly and quickly when we are in a difficult situation we shall be delivered out of it much sooner.

Zechariah: 9 verse 17   Aug 15

For how great is His goodness and how great is His beauty!

How can we comprehend the beauty of God, He must be magnificent. With Jesus sitting at His right hand side surrounded by Glory. Also with Angels singing Holy, Holy, Holy is the LORD. His beauty must be incredible.

James: 5 verse 13   Aug 16

Is any one of you in trouble? He should pray. Is anyone happy? Let him sing songs of praise.

Today have we sung a song unto The Lord? Do you know that He loves us to sing? Now is a good time to begin. God gave us each a voice and He does love to hear each one of us sing. So rejoice in our God, do not be ashamed of your voice. If you belong to God, your voice really belongs to Him. Allelujah!

Proverbs: 11 verse 11   Aug 17

Through the blessing of the upright a city is exalted but by the mouth of the wicked it is destroyed.

Just think right where you are, you can be a blessing to the city or town that you live in. In your own communi- ty you can be a blessing, by praying and being in the love Jesus day by day. We are not all called to go out to be a prominent person in our community but by prayer and supplication we as Christians can make a great dif- ference in the city around us. Today let us pray for the place that we live in, for peace to prevail and for the mouth of the wicked to by cleansed.

Matthew: 5 verse 8   Aug 18

Blessed are the pure in heart, for they will see God.

Oh! to be pure in heart and see God. Today let us ask God to show us some of the bad things in our heart so that we can get rid of them. So our hearts can become purer for Jesus.

Mark: 5 verse 28   Aug 19

Because she though, "If I just touch His clothes, I will be healed"

That was the woman with the issue of blood speaking. As you know, yes, she was healed. We cannot touch Jesus clothes now as He is in Heaven. By faith though we can still be healed, through prayer. Jesus is still our healer today as He was 2000 years ago.

Ask God to allow Jesus to heal you today. Praise God He healed me. I pray that you receive your healing. Amen.

Psalm: 84 verse 10   Aug 20

Better is one day in your courts than a thousand
elsewhere; I would rather be a doorkeeper
in the house of my God than dwell
in the tents of the wicked.

That is true for me how about you?

Luke: 1 verse 76   Aug 21

And you, my child, will be called a prophet of the Most High; for you will go on before The Lord to prepare the way for Him.

This was part of Zechariah's Song after the birth of his son John. Now we can't all be prophet's as you know but we can in our own way prepare the way of The Lord. How you may ask, well, we can sing praises (the devil doesn't like that, he has to get out of the way) so that helps to prepare the way, we can pray, we can do lots of things. This is a good day to ask The Lord what He would especially like you to do to prepare the way for Him today. Jesus will bless you as you serve Him.

2Peter: 3 verse 18　　　　　　　　　　　　Aug 22

But grow in the grace and knowledge of our Lord and Saviour Jesus Christ. To Him be glory both now and forever! Amen.

Isn't lovely to think that we can grow in the grace and the knowledge of our Lord Jesus. Today as we learn and read more about Him let us ask God Our Father to allow us more grace to really know His Son Jesus, our Saviour, more and more. Amen.

James: 3 verse 13　　　　　　　　　　　　Aug 23

Who is wise and understanding among you? Let him show it by his good life, by deeds done in the humility that comes from wisdom.

Today we can have a good life as we walk in wisdom and humility. Yes we do need understanding, if we ask—remember we shall receive, so let us ask especially today for more understanding of God's ways and of His word.

Proverbs: 19 verse 4   Aug 24

Wealth brings many friends but a poor man's friend deserts him.

Sometimes that can seem very true but remember as a Christian there is one friend who will never desert you and that is Jesus. Do you really realise that He loves you so much that He died on the cross even for you. It is hard for me to comprehend the great love that He as even for me. God Bless you today as you meditate on these things.

Hebrews: 13 verse 5   Aug 25

Keep your lives free from the love of money and be content with what you have, because God has said,

"Never will I leave you; never will I forsake you"

> Today that is still true, God's
> word stands forever!
> Amen.

Psalm: 115 verse 1 — Aug 26

> Not to us, O LORD, not to us but
> to Your name be the glory,
> because of Your love and faithfulness.

I give you the glory today O LORD. Because of your love and faithfulness to me, I thank you for all your blessings to me. I am so blessed by you and by Jesus and by your Holy Spirit.

Philemon: verse 4 — Aug 27

I always thank my God as I remember you in my prayers.

It is good to know that someone remembers us in their prayers and how marvellous to know that God hears us when we pray for each other. So today is the day maybe, to pray for someone different that you have never prayed for before. Remember them in your prayers, perhaps a neighbour or a friend. Ask God to show you someone new to pray for today.

What a blessing you can be to that person.

Psalm: 79 verse 8 — Aug 28

> Do not hold against us the sins of the fathers; may Your mercy come quickly to meet us, for we are in desperate need.

Sometimes we do feel in desperate need, and we muddle on in our self-pity and in the sins of our fathers, until at last we remember to pray. If only today we shall remember to pray quickly for whatever need arises instead of trying to get on with things our own way. Because as the Psalm says God's mercy does come quickly to us. - He does like us to ask Him though!

Titus: 2 verses 7 - 8 — Aug 29

In everything set them an example by doing what is good. In your teaching show integrity, seriousness and soundness of speech that cannot be condemned, so that those who oppose you may be ashamed because they have nothing bad to say about us.

Each day and that includes today we need to set an example by doing what is good. There is a lot to think about in the above verses. Today let us watch carefully what we say and how we teach, especially in our own families. May the joy of The Lord fill your heart as you start afresh today.

2 Timothy: 1 v 7   Aug 30

For God did not give us a spirit of timidity but a spirit of power, of love and of self-discipline

I praise you today God for the spirit of love and power that you have given to me. The spirit of self-discipline in me is only active because of your love and power. Thank you God, thank you.

Psalm: 137 verse 6   Aug 31

May my tongue cling to the roof of my mouth if I do not remember you, if I do not consider Jerusalem my highest joy.

Jerusalem is Your Holy City God and I await in expectation with all the family of God to see the New Jerusalem. Your City paved with Gold, with no darkness, aglow with the light of The Lamb. Amen.

***

Psalm 1

1 Blessed is the man that walketh not in the counsel of the ungodly, nor standeth in the way of sinners, nor sitteth in the seat of the scornful.
2 But his delight is in the Law of The LORD; and in His law doth he mediate day and night.
3 And he shall be like a tree planted by the rivers of water, that bringeth forth his fruit in his season; his leaf also shall not wither; and whatsoever he doeth shall prosper.
4 The ungodly are not so; but are like the chaff which the wind driveth away.
5 Therefore the ungodly shall not stand in the judgement, nor sinners in the congregation of the righteous.
6 For The LORD knoweth the way of the righteous; but the way of the ungodly shall perish.

Have you thought to look at a flower today,
to see how intricately they are made?
Take a special look and smell
the beautiful fragrance.
It is one more thing of beauty
that our God has made.

September

1 Peter: 2 verse 3 — Sept 1

Now that you have tasted that The Lord is Good.

Once that we have tasted that The Lord is Good, we really do want to know more about Him for sure. So I pray Lord Jesus that we do come to know you more as we go about our daily living today. Amen.

Philippians: 3 verse 8 — Sept 2

What is more, I consider everything a loss compared to the surpassing greatness of knowing Christ Jesus my Lord, for whose sake I have lost all things. I consider them rubbish, that I may gain Christ.

To lose all things often means that we must give up those things that we love and things that we love to do that are not worthy of God. They then have no hold on us, so that we can truly gain Jesus Christ as Lord in our lives. Is there anything that you need to let go of today that is accounted as an abomination to the Kingdom. i.e. idols, love of money, hate, anger, wrong friendships etc., etc., Ask God in your prayer time and He will show you so that you can become more pure each day in your heart.

Psalm: 78 verse 15 — Sept 3

> He split the rocks in the desert and gave
> them water as abundant as the seas;

That must have been an incredible sight. Think of the mighty things that our God does for us day by day. Small miracles, large miracles, He does miraculous things even today.

2 Timothy: 2 verse 11 — Sept 4

Here is a trustworthy saying:

If we died with Him, we will also live with Him

When we invite Jesus into our lives, we become new creatures in Christ. Our old selves have died and we become one with Him. Therefore praise The Lord we do live with Him today - also forever and ever. Amen.

2 Timothy: 2 verse 12 — Sept 5

If we endure, we will also reign with Him. If we disown Him He will also disown us;

Let us endure today, so that we can reign with Jesus, it would be dreadful to be disowned by our Saviour. Today let us give Him praise that is due to His holy name and revel in the love that He showers upon us.

2 Timothy: 2 verse 13 — Sept 6

If we are faithless, He will remain faithful, for He cannot disown Himself.

When we belong to Jesus and our faith seems to desert us, remember that He is still faithful to us. He is always there. Even today right this minute Jesus is faithful to us. Let us pray and ask that our faith be refreshed and renewed today. Amen.

Proverbs: 11 verse 17 — Sept 7

A kind man benefits himself but a cruel man brings trouble on himself.

Dear Lord God please help us to be kind today to all you bring before us and help me to be kind to myself. I thank you God for your never-ending kindness to me as insignificant as I am.

Psalm: 110 verse 1 — Sept 8

The LORD says to my Lord: "Sit at my right hand until I make your enemies a footstool for your feet"

Just think The LORD also makes our enemy Satan to be trampled under our feet. We do not have to put up with his lies, let us stand firm in the love of God and trample the enemy under our feet today. Remember though only as we walk with Jesus and pray in the spirit can we do this. Amen.

Galatians: 5 verse 16   Sept 9

So I say, live by the Spirit and you will not gratify the desires of the sinful nature.

Dear God help us today not to gratify those desires of the flesh that are not right by you. We do need your help God, we cannot do anything good by ourselves without You and Jesus, by the help of your Holy Spirit. Amen.

Genesis: 7 verse 2   Sept 10

Take with you seven of every kind of clean animal, a male and its mate and two of every kind of unclean animal, a male and its mate.

Today has been a revelation to realise that the animals didn't all go into the Ark - two of everything—but God asked Noah to take in seven of every kind of clean animal. Because when think about it Noah and his family needed food for themselves.

Genesis: 7 verse 3   Sept 11

And also seven of every kind of bird, male and female, to keep their various kinds alive throughout the earth.

How about that then, seven of every kind of bird, male and female. We have been brought up singing that song—(The animals went in two by two) - never checking what else God had said. Just taking it for granted that only two of each kind had gone into the Ark. But not so, as you can see. It makes me wonder, what else have we missed by not reading the Bible correctly, skipping over some bits and listening to other people tell us things, without checking them out.

Today is a good day to start reading and listening to God, being guided by The Holy Spirit, not just by man.

Psalm: 135 verse 5 — Sept 12

I know that The LORD is great, that our LORD is greater than all gods.

Yes we do know that our God is greater than all other gods. He is Almighty God, Creator of the Universe, The Ancient of Days, Our Father in Heaven, we know He is Great. Allelujah!

Luke: 8 verse 16 — Sept 13

"No one lights a lamp and hides it in a jar or puts it under a bed. Instead, he puts it on a stand, so that those who come in can see the light."

Today let us be like a lamp shining forth the light, the love of The Lord Jesus. Don't let us be forever hiding the light that is in us.

Colossians: 3 verse 1 — Sept 14

Since, then, you have been raised with Christ, set your hearts on things above, where Christ is seated at the right hand of God.

If only we could see Jesus seated at the right hand of God wouldn't it be marvellous. In faith, being born again into the Kingdom of God we shall see as we are seen. So today in faith let us praise God for Jesus Christ our saviour, putting our hearts on things above.

Psalm: 138 verse 8 — Sept 15

> The LORD will fulfil His purpose for me;
> your love, O LORD, endures for ever - do
> not abandon the works of your hands.

Today - please God continue to fulfil your purpose for me. I thank you that you will never leave me nor forsake me because your word tells me that in the Bible. Amen.

Psalm: 65 verse 4   Sept 16

> Blessed are those you choose and
> bring near to live in your courts!
> We are filled with the good things of
> your house, of your Holy Temple.

We praise you LORD God that you do choose us to be Christians, your chosen people. today I do want to be filled with all good things that you have for me.

Thank you God.

Matthew: 15 verses 19-20   Sept 17

For out of the heart come evil thoughts, murder, adultery, sexual immorality, theft, false testimony, slander. These are what make a man 'unclean' but eating with unwashed hands does not make him 'unclean'

As we travel through today let us let go of all evil thoughts, how can we ;possibly be 'clean' if we harbour hatred, jealousy, bitterness and strife in our hearts. Dear God please continue to cleanse me with the blood of The Lamb. Help me to banish all unclean things from my heart. Wash me clean Lord of all evil things today. Amen.

Colossians: 2 verse 6 — Sept 18

So then, just as you received Christ Jesus as Lord continue to live in Him.

Yes, today and forever I want to live in Jesus Christ my Saviour.

Proverbs: 16 v 3 — Sept 19

Commit to The Lord whatever you do and your plans will succeed.

The above saying is true, if we do commit our plans to The Lord, as long as they are in agreement with His ways then He will allow them to succeed. Have you tried committing your day to The Lord? If not why not have a go today!

Genesis: 19 verse 26 — Sept 20

But Lot's wife looked back and she became a pillar of salt.

Help me today Lord not to look back, as I am a Christian let me not want to be part of the life that I have left behind, the part of being a sinner. I am redeemed by Jesus help me to walk in the love of Jesus today please by the guiding of your Holy Spirit.

Psalm: 116: verse 1 — Sept 21

> I love The LORD, for He heard my
> voice; He heard my cry for mercy.

What would my life be without you LORD, you are my life, you did hear my cry. I praise you LORD with all my heart and soul and all that is within me. Amen.

Isaiah: 52 verse 7 — Sept 22

How beautiful on the mountains are the feet of those who bring good news,.....

Let our feet be those that take the good news of the gospel to our neighbours and friends and to those in the workplace. There are so many souls out there that do not know Jesus our Saviour. Even today we could possibly show the love of Jesus to someone, just a smile may help. Look at the faces around you as you go shopping or to and fro to work etc., a smile is such a little thing but it can mean so much.

Philippians: 4 verse 4 — Sept 23

Rejoice in the Lord always. I will say it again: Rejoice!

It is lovely to rejoice in The Lord, how much better we feel ourselves when we stop complaining and start rejoicing in all the marvellous things He does for us and already has done in our lives. So today let us Rejoice, Rejoice and be glad.

Psalm: 80 verse 19   Sept 24

Restore us, O LORD GOD Almighty; make
Your face shine upon us, that we may be saved.

Thank you LORD that you have allowed your face to shine on us and that as Christians now we have been saved. I pray that those who are in the world will allow you to shine your face on them and accept Jesus as their Saviour.

Hebrews: 10 verse 19   Sept 25

Therefore, brothers, since we have confidence to enter the Most Holy Place by the blood of Jesus........

It's good to read the next few verses in the Bible, of the above scripture to know that we have been cleansed by the blood of Jesus to enter into that Most Holy Place. For us to pray directly to our Heavenly Father, through Jesus Christ our Lord. So today have confidence to come before God as one of His children to pray for your needs, then give Him the Glory that He is entitled to. Because there is no-one like our God. He is Almighty God the one and only true God maker of Heaven and earth. Amen.

Isaiah: 52 verse 13 — Sept 26

See, my servant will act wisely; he will be raised and lifted up and highly exalted.

We are servants of the most high God, when we act wisely - yes even us - you and me, we are lifted up in God's eyes and He does exalt us. Dear God please help me to act wisely today in all circumstances so that I do feel lifted up. Amen.

Psalm: 136 verse 26 — Sept 27

> Give thanks to the God of heaven.
> His love endures for ever.

Thank you LORD God that your love does endure forever and ever especially also to myself thank you.

God gave us hands to use for
prayer and friendship.
Let us use our hands to praise God today for
His goodness to us.

John: 11 verse 11 — Sept 28

After He had said this, He went on to tell them, "Our friend Lazarus has fallen asleep; but I am going there to wake him up"

How many of us have just about fallen asleep in our sins and are not doing the work that we should be doing for Jesus? It was Jesus who spoke those words above, maybe we should ask Him to awake us from our slumber to work in a more awake manner for The Kingdom of God. Please wake us, shake us today Lord for The Kingdom's sake. Amen.

Psalm: 66 verse 20 — Sept 29

> Praise be to God, who has not rejected my prayer or withheld His love from me!

Thank you LORD God that you have not rejected me in any way and that you truly love even me. Amen.

Job: 4 verse 17 — Sept 30

Can a mortal be more righteous than God? Can a man be more pure than his Maker?

Oh! that we should ever dare to think such a thing. That was what Satan thought and look where it landed him.

Let us be glad that we have such a wonderful Maker - Our Heavenly Father and give Him all the praise and glory that we can today and for always Amen.

***

October

Philippians: 4 verse 11 — Oct 1

I am not saying this because I am in need, for I have learned to be content whatever the circumstances.

Today is the start of a new month, let us endeavor to be content if we can this month in whatever circumstances we find ourselves. Let us rest in the knowledge and love of Jesus that He is with us everyday, comforting and guiding us by His Holy Spirit.

Psalm: 109 verse 4 — Oct 2

> In return for my friendship they accuse
> me but I am a man of prayer.

Sometimes our friends do accuse us, they do not always understand us when we try to help them. But as long as we pray for them the Lord will intervene and bless the situation. Today and everyday we need to be a man (or a woman) of prayer.

Matthew: 20 verse 14 — Oct 3

Take your pay and go. I want to give the man who was hired last the same as I gave you.

Most of us in our hearts are selfish, we are not happy to see that someone who has not worked as long as us receive the same blessings, anointing, knowledge etc., as we have. Whoever comes into God's Kingdom in these last days are entitled to all the same things that The Lord has given us. They will not have to work

and learn all the years that we have done. Because through us as Spirit Filled Christians, The Lord will cause the new Christians to accept quickly, almost straightaway the blessings that He has. So the one that was hired last Jesus is entitled to give even the same that we have now.

Philippians: 4 verse 13   Oct 4

I can do all things through Christ who strengthens me.

Do you know we really can! As long as we put our trust in Jesus, God will strengthen us day by day. Thank you LORD that you do strengthen us by your Holy Spirit who is in us. Amen.

Proverbs: 31 verse 8   Oct 5

"Speak up for those who cannot speak for themselves, for the rights of all who are destitute"

We do need to speak for those who cannot speak for themselves, especially the little children, the babies, the unborn that people want to abort. Speak for those who cannot speak, pray for them, don't let the devil have them. Pray for those in the world who are destitute, that they may come to know Jesus today.

Psalm: 61 verse 4 — Oct 6

> I long to dwell in your tent forever
> and take refuge in the shelter of your wings.

What a lovely thought to dwell with The LORD forever in the shelter of His love.

Philippians: 4 verse 19 — Oct 7

And my God will meet all your needs according to His glorious riches in Christ Jesus.

I pray that my God is your God today, that you have invited Christ Jesus into your heart so that you are born again and can live in the glorious riches that God has for all who believe and acknowledge Jesus as Lord. May The Lord Jesus bless you richly today.

Genesis: 2 verse 2 — Oct 8

And God blessed the seventh day and made it Holy, because on it He rested from all the work of creating that He had done.

We must choose one day a week to have as our Sabbath, to rest from our work and use as a Holy Day for The Lord. Everyone cannot choose a Saturday or a Sunday according to the work they do but one day should be chosen as a rest day to honour God.

Exodus: 16 verse 9   Oct 9

Then Moses told Aaron, "Say to the entire Israelite community, Come before The LORD, for He has heard your grumbling"

Even today do you know that The LORD can hear our grumbling? Yes He can! Let us try to get though the day without a grumble. Well, we can try and with the help of The Holy Spirit - we should hopefully make it.

Psalm: 81 verse 9   Oct 10

> You shall have no foreign god among you,
> you shall not bow down to an alien god.

As Christians we acknowledge the one and only true God, Our Father in Heaven. So today we may be able to let others know about Him. What a blessing it will be for them to come to know The Kingdom of God.

Proverbs; 2 verse 10   Oct 11

For Wisdom will enter your heart and knowledge will be pleasant to your soul.

I pray today that Wisdom will enter into our hearts more than is already there. That we shall rejoice in the new knowledge that The Lord will reveal, also that it will truly be pleasant and a joy to our soul. Amen.

Psalm: 150 verse 6   Oct 12

> Let everything that has breath praise
> The LORD. Praise The LORD.

Well, what about us today - we have breath, so let us praise The LORD. With all our heart and soul we praise you LORD God our Heavenly Father, for being who you are, our Almighty God, maker of the Universe, ruler over all. Amen.

Hebrews: 1 verse 6   Oct 13

And again, when God brings His first-born into the world, He says, "Let all God's angels worship Him"

How much more then should we worship Jesus God's own beloved Son. Sometimes our praise seems so inadequate for all the things Jesus did for us when He came to earth. But our combined praise as we praise together throughout the world must surely be worthy and acceptable to Him. We praise you and worship you Lord Jesus today for all your love toward us.

Genesis: 1 verse 31   Oct 14

God saw all that He had made and it was very good. And there was evening and there was morning the sixth day.

God made everything good in this world and you can see by the above that He knew it was good. Evening is the start of the day according to the above verse, that really gives us food for thought, something to think about doesn't it?

Psalm: 111 verse 10   Oct 15

> The fear of The LORD is the beginning
> of wisdom; all who follow His precepts
> have good understanding.
> To Him belongs Eternal Praise.

Do we have the beginning of wisdom today? Let us hope so, then we shall begin to understand our Heavenly Father more and more each day, not being fearful but having a reverent respect and fear of Him, following His precepts and walking in His love.

Leviticus: 19 verses 1 - 2   Oct 16

The LORD said to Moses, "Speak to the entire assembly of Israel and say to them: "Be holy because I, the LORD your God, am Holy.

Today we need to be reminded of this - we need to be holy because The LORD our God is Holy How can we do this you may well ask? Possibly in lots of ways but one thing we can do, is to try to keep ourselves from the evils of this world. God has called us to be holy. That means we are set aside for Him. Let us try to stay that way for The LORD our God each day.

Psalm: 82 verse 1   Oct 17

God presides in the great assembly; He gives judgement among the "gods"

Just think our God judges all the other "gods" How much ore will He need to judge us? Let us praise The LORD that He allows Jesus to intercede at His right hand for us, His chosen people today.

Thank you Jesus that you intercede for me. Amen.

2 Timothy: 1 verse 7   Oct 18

For God did not give us a spirit of timidity but a spirit of power, of love and self-discipline.

Today we need to remember these things that God has given us - so that we can be more holy and powerful in prayer for Him.

Psalm: 145 verse 15 — Oct 19

> The eyes of all look to You and You give
> them their food at the proper time.

Yes LORD you feed us all, you have given us the fruits of the earth. The animals are all catered for. The birds of the air and the fish in the sea. It is incredible the wondrous things You have done. You have programed our bodies to know when it is time to be fed and you supply all our needs. Thank you God.

Mark: 10 verse 6 — Oct 20

> But at the beginning of Creation God 'made them male and female'

Today let us rejoice that God made us the way we are. He made us either male or female. So what ever sex you are honour the fact that God loves you just as you are, don't try to change. Be the man or woman that you were destined to be. Ask God to help you to be the person He wants.

Luke: 8 verse 17 — Oct 21

> For there is nothing hidden that will not be disclosed and nothing concealed that will not be known or brought out into the open.

So there we are, we best not conceal things from God. We must bring things out into the light. If we have hidden anything in our hearts that is not Godly, let us bring it before Jesus and ask forgiveness, then it is in the light and Jesus does forgive us our sins, the Bible tells us so. Praise God.

Psalm: 113 verse 4   Oct 22

> The LORD is exalted over all the nations,
> His glory above the heavens.

We praise you LORD that you are exalted over all the nations on this earth. We praise you for your glory that is above the heavens and pray that we may soon see more and more of your glory here on this planet earth. Amen.

Luke: 8 verse 25   Oct 23

"Where is your faith?" He asked His disciples. In fear and amazement they asked one another. "Who is this? He commands even the winds and the water and they obey Him."

So where is our faith today? God has anointed us to do great things in the name of Jesus our Saviour - are we ready in our faith to accomplish that which God wants us to do today? I pray dear God that you will enable me with the faith that I have to be an overcomer for Jesus sake today. Amen.

Isaiah: 50 verse 7 — Oct 24

Because the Sovereign LORD helps me, I will not be disgraced. Therefore have I set my face like flint and I know I will not be put to shame.

Know today that The LORD will help you in all circumstances. You do not have to open your mouth to those who oppose you, pray to The LORD our God and He will vindicate you. Stand firm in your faith knowing that He is near.

Romans: 6 verse 5 — Oct 25

If we have been united with Him like this in His death, we will certainly also be united with Him in His resurrection.

Just think of the marvellous day when we go home to be with Jesus our Lord and Saviour. Only if we belong to Jesus can we go to that marvellous place when we leave our earthly bodies. Thank you Lord.

Psalm: 112 verse 1 — Oct 26

Praise The LORD. Blessed is the man who fears The LORD, who finds great delight in His commands.

Let us find great delight in God's commands today, one of which is love your neighbour. Let us try to find delight in our neighbours, i.e. the people around about us today. Please LORD help me to be a blessing to all you bring before me today. Amen.

Revelation: 7 verse 16   Oct 27

Never again will they hunger, never again will they thirst. The sun will not bear upon them, nor any scorching heat.

This is for all who acknowledge Jesus as Lord when we go to be with Him forever and ever. Sit and think for a moment, of our great inheritance as saints of the living God.

Jude: verse 18   Oct 28

They said to you, "in the last times there will be scoffers who will follow their own ungodly desires."

Please help me today God not to follow my own ungodly desires. May your Holy spirit guide me into all righteousness and truth Amen.

Proverbs: 25 verse 21   Oct 29

If your enemy is hungry, give him food to eat; if he is thirsty, give him water to drink.

This may seem a bit odd to do this but the LORD will surely bless you when you do it. Remember we are not to judge! That is for The lord to do, so we best feed and water even those who come against us.

3 John: 1 verse 11　　　　　　　　　　　Oct 30

Dear friend, do not imitate what is evil but what is good. Anyone who does what is good is from God. Anyone who does what is evil has not seen God.

Today let us not grow weary of doing good! That is a word The Lord gave me when I got a bit fed up one day and thought what is the good of trying to help whoever it was. Then the quiet voice of The Holy Spirit said "Jessie never weary of doing good" so I pass that on to you today, please don't grow tired of doing good. God

is good. He is love, He is all goodness. He is The LORD!

2 John: 1 verse 4　　　　　　　　　　　Oct 31

I has given me great joy to find some of your children walking in the truth, just as The Father commanded us.

It would give our Heavenly Father great joy to find our children walking in the truth of Jesus. Let us today be a good example to our children and also to other children in the world so that they too may come to know Jesus as their Lord and Saviour. May The Lord Jesus bless you today as you walk with God.

Amen.

***

November

> *God*
> *is*
> *Love*

<u>Are You a Ripple on a Pond.</u>

Are you a Ripple on a Pond?
Do you see what I see?
Can you pray for those who cannot pray? Will
you pray for those who cannot see?

Are you a Ripple on a Pond.?
Like a pebble thrown into the middle, our
prayers can go out and around
in a never ending and expanding circle.

Are you a ripple on a pond? Do you see beyond the horizon?
Will your words or works reach out in
that never ending circle of prayer?

I pray I am a Ripple on a Pond.
My prayers going forth throughout the world,
for those lost souls to be gathered in
and for everyone of them to be cleansed from sin.

Do try to be a Ripple,
even starting with a trickle, of prayer and praise.
Like a pebble creating waves on a Pond, may
your Prayers go forward even beyond.

So are you a Ripple on a Pond?
With prayers, reach far beyond all that you see.
Look and use your spiritual eyes for Jesus.
Do something for Him that really, really pleases.

Psalm: 70 verse 4 — Nov 1

> But may all who seek you rejoice
> and be glad in you; may those who
> love your Salvation always say,
> "Let God be exalted"

Today I seek you LORD God to say that I love you and that I love your Salvation. I exalt you LORD through Jesus Christ my Lord and by your Holy Spirit I know that I can praise and exalt you.

Hebrews: 1 verse 14 — Nov 2

Are not all angels ministering spirits sent to serve those who will inherit Salvation.

Let us thank God our Heavenly Father for allowing His angels to care for us, that they minister to us in ways we cannot see but they are there serving and helping us whenever the need arises. Thank you God.

Proverbs: 18 verse 10 — Nov 3

The name of The LORD is a strong tower; the righteous run to it and are safe.

I am so glad LORD God that I can come to you at anytime and feel safe in your love and care. Even right now today I know that you are there and in control of everything. Help me please to continue in righteousness. Amen.

John: 4 verse 34 — Nov 4

"My food," said Jesus, "is to do the will of Him who sent me and to finish His work"

This is what we need to say as well, that our food is truly our work for God. When we work for God we feel content and filled with goodness. Let us try to finish the work that He wants us to do so that we shall feel fed with Heavenly food.

Psalm: 75 verse 2 — Nov 5

> You say, "I choose the appointed time,
>   it is I who judge uprightly"

Yes LORD it is you who chooses the appointed time for all things. You judge uprightly. You know all things. You know our going out and our coming in. Thank you that you are my God and my judge, that you correct me at the right time in all things.

John: 4 verse 37 — Nov 6

Thus the saying 'One sows and another reaps' is true.

Lots of us are meant to be sowers of the seed, that is sowers of the word of the Gospel of The Lord Jesus Christ. Have you sown any seed yet for The Kingdom? How lovely for God to have a harvest of our fruit from the seeds that we have sown! Let us begin to sow in readiness for a great harvest of souls.

Psalm: 46 verse 10   Nov 7

"Be still and know that I am God;
I will be exalted among the nations,
I will be exalted in the earth"

Have you ever sat still for a while and felt the presence of God. Be still and know. that is what He wants us to do. As we sit with The Holy spirit how lovely is the presence of God.

Colossians: 1 verse 12   Nov 8

Giving thanks to The Father, who has qualified you to share in the inheritance of the saints in The Kingdom of Light.

I give thanks to you my Heavenly Father that you have qualified me through Jesus Christ your Son to share in the inheritance of the saints in your Kingdom of Light. Amen.

Psalm: 72 verse 19   Nov 9

Praise be to His glorious name for ever; may the whole earth be filled with His glory.
Amen and Amen.

I pray today LORD God that soon we shall see the whole earth filled with Your Glory, that Jesus will come back soon and Your Glory be revealed more and more. Amen.

Titus: 1 verse 15   Nov 10

To the pure, all things are pure but to those who are corrupted and do not believe, nothing is pure. In fact, both their minds and consciences are corrupted.

Dear God help me to be more pure. Don't let me allow myself to be corrupt in any way today. Amen.

Psalm: 76 verse 4   Nov 11

You are resplendent with light, more majestic than mountains rich with game.

How can we comprehend Your majesty, Your holy light, Your Heavenly Throne? Heavenly Father God none can come near Your resplendent light. You are Almighty God. Today we honour You for all Your love and care for us.

Proverbs: 11 verse 11   Nov 12

Through the blessing of the upright a City is exalted but by the mouth of the wicked it is destroyed.

I ask for blessings today LORD for the City that I am in, right here God in this place. I ask that you exalt this place so that it will begin to be holy for You. Amen.

Psalm: 73 verse 28   Nov 13

> But as for me it is good to be near God.
> I have made the Sovereign LORD my
> refuge, I will tell of all your deeds.

Yes, God I will tell of Your deeds toward me, that you have healed my body from an incurable disease. You have saved me by the blood of Jesus, so that I can live in Your Kingdom forever and ever. Amen.

2 Timothy: 1 verse 8   Nov 14

So do not be ashamed to testify about our Lord, or ashamed of me His prisoner. But join with me in suffering for the gospel, by the power of God.

It was Paul who said the above and it is so relevant for us today not to be ashamed to suffer for the Gospel of

Christ. Nor to be embarrassed or ashamed to testify about those things that God has done for us in our life.

Psalm: 123 verse 2 — Nov 15

As the eyes of slaves look to the hand of their master,
as the eyes of a maid look to the hand
of her mistress, so our eyes look to
The LORD our God, till He shows us His mercy.

That is just what we need to do isn't it? We need to look to God our heavenly Father when we have a special need and wait for His mercy to be with us and help us in the situation. However our eyes must look to God, not all over the place to other people who cannot possibly help us in the way that God can, in His special love and mercy. So take courage today and pray to God for that special need that you have, wait on Him and you will see the answer to your prayers.

Hebrews: 3 verse 1 — Nov 16

Therefore, holy brothers, who share in the heavenly calling, fix your thoughts on Jesus, the apostle and high priest whom we confess.

This really is a reminder today that we pray to the Father through Jesus Christ His Son. With the help of The Holy Spirit we can pray and ask for whatever our needs are. If we pray according to God's will, He will grant our individual special needs.

Psalm: 125 verse 2 — Nov 17

As the mountains surround Jerusalem, so The LORD surrounds His people both now and for evermore.

Imagine today that The LORD is surrounding you, yes you have angels around you guarding you, also your own specially appointed guardian angel. Praise The LORD that He cares so much about all of us who belong to His Kingdom.

Proverbs: 13 verse 24 — Nov 18

He who spares the rod hates his son but he who loves him is careful to discipline him.

This does not mean that we should go about hitting our children with a rod until they cower before us. It does mean that we must discipline them in a way that they will understand not to do that bad thing again. As children of God did you know that God disciplines us? Because He loves us He is constantly correcting us, that is how it should be with us and our natural children. They must not be allowed to do just as they like, when and how they like, neither can we in God's Kingdom. Today let us rejoice that Our Father in Heaven loves us so much that He disciplines us with love.

Matthew: 7 verse 1   Nov 19

Do not judge, or you too will be judged.

We must be very careful not to judge each other, because the manner in which we judge them, we too shall be judged by our Heavenly Father. Today please Holy Spirit help us not to judge anyone to be unrighteously. Amen.

Psalm: 69 verse 30   Nov 20

> I will praise God's name in song and
> glorify Him with thanksgiving.

Dear Lord I love to sing to you, especially with your Holy Spirit singing in me and through me so that I can glorify your Holy Name with thanksgiving in my heart today and everyday.

Matthew: 6 verse 3   Nov 21

But when you give to the needy, do not let your left hand know what your right hand is doing.

Please remember that as we give to the needy, we do not have to tell others about it. Because we could be inviting a spirit of pride to come into us. Today let us give according to God's word with the love of Jesus.

Proverbs: 11 verse 25   Nov 22

A generous man will prosper; he who refreshes others will himself be refreshed.

Thank you so much dear God that this verse is so true please allow me to refresh and help someone for you today. Amen.

Psalm: 124 verse 7   Nov 23

We have escaped like a bird out of the fowler's snare; the snare has been broken and we have escaped.

Yes LORD we have escaped out the fowler's snare, you have graciously brought us into your Kingdom of love through Jesus Christ our Lord, your only beloved Son. Thank you LORD God.

Proverbs: 13 verse 15   Nov 24

Good understanding wins favour but the way of the unfaithful is hard.

Thank you God that you allow us to have understanding in our hearts with faith and a great love for Jesus our Lord, so that we can win your favour even today. Amen.

Proverbs: 11 verse 13   Nov 25

A gossip betrays a confidence but a trustworthy man keeps a secret.

We know that only with the help of Jesus can we truly keep a secret. Please help us Lord not to gossip, curb our tongue please and let your Holy Spirit speak through even my tongue today Amen.

Psalm: 122 verse 6   Nov 26

> Pray for the peace of Jerusalem:
> "May those who love You
> be secure"

Let us not forget to pray for Jerusalem, the Holy City, where Jesus will be coming back to Zion His Holy Hill. As we pray, we can feel secure in the love of God our Father and Jesus His Son. So pray today for the peace of Jerusalem, be glad that God is in control of everything.

Proverbs: 12 verse 28   Nov 27

In the way of righteousness there is life; along that path is immortality.

Today is another day for us to walk in righteousness, to walk in true life on our way to immortality, to Eternity.

Walk in righteousness with Jesus today, tell Him you love Him and look forward to the day when we walk in Heaven with Him.

1 Peter: 5 verse 13   **Nov 28**

Is any one of you in trouble? He should pray. Is anyone happy? Let him sing songs of praise.

Well are you in trouble today? Are you happy today? Are you singing songs of praise? Whatever place you seem to be in today, it is the right time to pray. We can pray without ceasing, let us pray.

Psalm: 127 verse 1   **Nov 29**

> Unless The LORD builds the house,
> it's builders labour in vain.

Our body is the house (the temple of God) for The Holy Spirit to dwell in. today God please continue to build my house, my body, for your Holy Spirit of Jesus to dwell in and use for your glory now and forever while I live on this earth. Amen.

Luke: 8 verse 24   **Nov 30**

The disciples went and woke Him, saying, "Master, Master, we're going to drown"

He got up and rebuked the wind and the raging waters; the storm subsided and all was calm.

Call on Jesus today. Know that He will not let you drown and that the same Spirit that was in Him to rebuke the wind and the waves is in everyone who is born again into Jesus Christ, into the Kingdom of God. So today is a good day to invite Jesus into your heart if you have not already done so. And if you have, I say God Bless and keep you in the love of Jesus our Lord and Saviour. Amen.

***

December

Psalm: 77 verse 14 — Dec 1

> You are the God who performs miracles; You
> display Your power among the peoples.

Thank you God for all the miracles that you have done. those you are performing in these days, also for all the miracles that are to come. Thank you especially for the miracle of healing me of the incurable illness that I had, as well as other miraculous healings that you have sovereignly allowed me. Amen.

Psalm: 85 verse 13 — Dec 2

> Righteousness goes before Him and
> prepares the way for His steps.

Therefore if we are righteous before God today, it's a lovely thought that we are preparing the way for the coming of Jesus. Let us try to be kind and righteous to those around us today, in doing so we too shall be blessed.

Psalm: 2 verse 8 — Dec 3

> Ask of Me and I will make the Nations
> your inheritance,..................

When we pray for the Nations - The LORD God hears. Let us ask for the Nations to come into

Salvation. We can pray that way. God says ask of Me. Let us ask of Him today and pray for the Nations to be our inheritance that they all will come into God's Kingdom of light.

Psalm: 89 verse 15 — Dec 4

Blessed are those who have learned to acclaim you, who walk in the light of your presence,
O LORD.

Dear LORD I acclaim you today - you are my God. I love to walk in the light of your presence. To feel your wonderful peace and love around me. Thank you that you are my God.

Psalm: 141 verse 3 — Dec 5

Set a guard over my mouth, O LORD,
keep watch over the door of my lips.

Sometimes I think it is a good thing to ask The LORD to put a guard over my mouth to stop me saying something wrong and then wishing that I had not said it. As Christians we must be very careful what we say to others so that we do not offend them because in doing so we offend God if we do not speak righteously. Today please God guard my mouth, the door of my lips and my speaking. Amen.

Romans: 8 verses 1 - 2   **Dec 6**

Therefore, there is now no condemnation for those who are in Christ Jesus, because through Christ Jesus the law of the Spirit of life set me free from the law of sin and death.

Through the death of Jesus on the cross all of us who believe on Jesus are saved and are truly set free from the law of sin and death. As Jesus lives and reigns on high so do we live in Him. Amen

Psalm: 86 verse 4   **Dec 7**

Bring joy to your servant, for to you,
O LORD, I lift up my soul.

Today I lift up my soul to you my God. I look forward to receiving your joy today. You are my God. I do serve you my Father in Heaven. I am one of your adopted Son's living as a Christian on this earth. I look forward to your blessing of joy for me today.

Psalm: 139 verse 15   **Dec 8**

My frame was not hidden from you when I was made in the secret place.

God made us specially in that secret place, we must be very precious to Him. Today let us ask if there is anything special that He would like us to do for Him instead of asking for something for ourselves. He must be so pleased when the creatures that He has made show respect and love for Him and His Kingdom.

Psalm; 90 verse 2   Dec 9

> Before the mountains were born or You brought forth the earth and the world, from everlasting to everlasting You are God.

Praise You LORD God that you brought each one of us forth to become Children and Sons of God.

Psalm: 142 verse 7   Dec 10

> Set me free from my prison, that I may praise your name. Then the righteous will gather about me because of your goodness to me.

How often do we cry - set me free God from this place that I am in. One day I said to The LORD, "what is the point of all this I feel as if I am in a prison" Then the gentle voice of The Holy Spirit said - "and what did the disciples do when they were in prison" Do you know what they did? - They sung songs of praise!!! Look around and see what a beautiful prison you may be in, count your blessings then begin to sing. Praise The LORD, let us today not to ask to be set free, because, in the spirit we are free indeed. Amen.

In the spirit as Christians we are set free, to soar with the eagle on wings of praise.

Psalm: 104 verse 2 — Dec 11

> He wraps Himself in light as with a garment;
> He stretches out the Heavens like a tent.

Here we see that God wraps Himself in light, this true isn't it? He is the God of light. Moses could not look upon God and neither can we. But we can look toward the light and feel blessed as He wraps His light around us. Just like a garment we can feel the presence of The Holy Spirit who is The Sprit of Jesus our Lord who comes from The Father of Lights. Our God. Today let us ask to feel the garment of light around us.

Psalm: 133 verse 1 — Dec 12

> How good and pleasant it is when
> brothers live together in unity!

It is pleasant isn't it when we live together in unity! But sometimes we wonder how long will it last. Well, with us doing our bit to live in love and be at peace with our family and friends, it is amazing what God will do. So today let us do our part by living in unity and peace with all who come before us, with the Lord's help yes, we can have a good and pleasant day.

1 Colossians: 4 verse 6   Dec 13

Let your conversation be always full of grace, seasoned with salt, so that you may know how to answer everyone.

That is a lovely thought, to know how to answer everyone. But sometimes we really are not sure how to answer everyone are we? Today though, we can call on God our Heavenly Father to allow The Holy Spirit to have charge of our speaking so that we can answer with grace. Let us be like Jesus and wait on The LORD for the right answer before we speak wrongly. Then even our conversation can be full of wisdom - i.e. seasoned with salt.

Psalm: 143 verse 8   Dec 14

> Let the morning bring me word of your unfailing love, for I have put my trust in you. Show me the way I should go, for to You I lift up my soul.

Today I lift up my soul to You LORD God, please show me the way that I should go, I put my trust in You and in your unfailing love. So please show me the way for today, where you want me to go, what you want me to do. I wait on you now that morning is here. I look forward to doing something nice for you today God and for Jesus with the help of Your Holy Spirit. Amen.

Psalm: 88 verse 1   Dec 15

> O LORD, the God who saves me, day
> and night I cry out before you.

Yes I do cry out before you God. I need your help today and forever more. I am happy to cry out to You because you are my God and I know that you love me and that you hear my prayers.

> Thank you dear God.

Proverbs: 20 verse 7   Dec 16

The righteous man leads a blameless life; blessed are his children after him.

I really would like my children to be blessed because of my righteous life. I do try God to walk a blameless life for You but it is very difficult sometimes, especially when I forget to ask for your guidance and help. Today however I will start afresh, with your help to be the righteous person that you want me to be. Thank you that you sent Jesus to show us the way. Amen.

Psalm: 11 verse 4   Dec 17

> The LORD is in His Holy Temple; The LORD
> is on His Heavenly Throne. He observes the
> sons of men; His eyes examine them.

Today I want your eyes to examine me LORD to see if there is any wicked way in me. If there is, I want you to tell me so that I can become more righteous for you. So that I can walk in those heavenly places with Jesus Christ my Lord and feel no shame. Let your Holy Spirit who is my comforter and guide help me today in everyway to cleanse this earthen vessel.

Amen.

Job: 1 verse 21 Dec 18

"Naked I came from my mother's womb and naked I shall depart. The LORD gave and the LORD has taken away; may the name of The LORD be praised"

The above was said by Job and it is true, naked we came into this world and naked we shall leave it. So while we are here let us bless those around us as best we can, especially our family. Let us see them enjoy some of the assets we would eventually leave them when we die by giving now while we are alive. Let us share in their enjoyment. Maybe it could be just a special little heirloom we are saving for them or maybe finance we are saving for them. If they are in need as some young families are, let us be gracious and try to help. Today let us remember - we cannot take anything with us when we go, that also includes our love........

let them know you love them. Our families do need our love more than maybe they or we realise. The LORD surely blesses us as we bless others. Today let us think on our nakedness before The LORD.

Psalm: 147 verse 4   **Dec 19**

> He determines the number of the stars
> and calls them each by name.

Today let us remember that God calls us each by name. When we belong to Him He knows us, sees us, hears us. He knows our hearts, our souls, our needs, better than we know ourselves. So today maybe we can resubmit ourselves to Him and know for sure that yes He even knows our name.

<u>Psalm: 140 verse 121</u>   **Dec 20**

> Know that The LORD secures justice for the
> poor and upholds the cause of the needy.

If you are in any kind of need today please call on The LORD our God who will surely hear you and supply the special help that you need. Remember He knows your name and loves you.

Psalm: 103 verse 8   Dec 21

> The LORD is compassionate and gracious,
> slow to anger, abounding in love.

Today I would like to try to be more like The LORD, that is more compassionate and gracious toward others and slow to anger and I would definitely like to be abounding in love of The LORD to be able to give that love out to others. Help me today please LORD to be more Christ like, more like Jesus. Amen.

Psalm: 66 verse 20   Dec 22

> Praise be to God, who has not rejected my
> prayer or withheld His love from me!

I am so glad LORD God that you have not withheld your love from me. You hear my prayers, you are my God. You have healed me in my spirit, soul, mind and body and I am most grateful to you God, to Jesus and to The Holy Ghost, who is with me forever and ever. Amen.

Titus: 3 verse 14   Dec 23

Our people must learn to devote themselves to doing what is good, in order that they may provide for daily necessities and not live unproductive lives.

Paul wrote the above to Titus, so it is just as if he is writing to us. Never let us tire of doing good. And today LORD God I pray may be a productive day on my part for your Kingdom. Amen.

Matthew: 1 verse 18   Dec 24

This is how the birth of Jesus Christ came about: His Mother Mary was pledged to be married to Joseph but before they came together, she was found to be with child through the Holy Spirit.

Mary must have been a beautiful young woman spiritually to be so obedient to God saying yes to what He asked of her. How many of us can truly say that we are obedient to submit ourselves to the ways of The LORD? Dear LORD God I pray today that I may be more obedient to your voice and not to my own wants. In being obedient to you I know that you will be blessing me even more than I can ever imagine. Thank you for Mary the Mother of my Saviour - Jesus Christ my Lord. Amen.

Matthew: 1 verse 21   Dec 25

She will give birth to a Son and you are to give him the name Jesus, because he will save His people from their sins.

I am so glad that Mary was obedient, because if she had not given birth to Jesus where would you and I be today? It does not bear to think about it! Praise God today for the birth of Jesus who also was obedient to Our Heavenly Father to the extent of dying on The Cross for yours and my sins. I praise you Heavenly Father that You allowed Your only Son Jesus to come to earth to save us from certain death. Thank You that we choose today to celebrate the Birth of Jesus Christ our Lord being born on this earth. Amen.

Psalm: 67 verse 3   Dec 26

> May the peoples praise You, O God;
> may all the peoples praise You.

I praise you God, I praise you God, thank you for

today. Thank you for my family, for my friends, for the blessings that you give me. Thank you God for everything, my health, my food, my clothes, my shelter, thank you God. I praise you today, I praise you. Amen.

Psalm: 134 verse 2   Dec 27

> Lift up your hands in the sanctuary
> and praise The LORD.

We had a practice yesterday praising The LORD, so to- day maybe we can raise up our hands and praise Him. Remember He is an all seeing God and can see us even where we are at the moment raising our hands to praise to Him. People all over the world are praising God. He lives I the midst of our praises and He reigns on high. Allelujah!

Psalm: 131 verse 1   Dec 28

> My heart is not proud, O LORD, my eyes are not haughty; I do not concern myself with great matters or things too wonderful for me.

If only we could say this today and mean it! Can I really say that my heart is not proud, that my eyes are not haughty. Can I really say that I do not concern myself with things that I shouldn't? I would like to think so but sometimes it is a fearful thing to ask The LORD to search our hearts about these matters isn't it? So today LORD I do ask you to show me and help me to overcome the things that I need to overcome. By your grace only can I do it, with the help of The Holy Spirit - The Spirit of Jesus.

Psalm: 150 verse 6   Dec 29

> Let everything that has breath praise The LORD.

We have been praising The LORD, thanking Him and talking to Him. How about singing to Him today. To praise Him in singing is a double blessing, it is like praying twice. To sing praises is so special, remember God gives us a garment of praise for the spirit of heaviness. So sing, sing and you will notice that the spirit of heaviness (that's if it's about you anytime) will have to flee away. Praise The LORD!

Psalm: 146 verse 2   Dec 30

> I will praise The LORD all my life; I will
> sing praise to my God as long as I live.

Yes, I will, I will. I will and no devil is going to stop me praising The LORD and I will sing, yes I will sing, praises to my God as long as I live. Amen.

If today you are ill, maybe you can't speak or sing out loud for any reason i.e. sore throat or any other thing remember we can sing inside of us, in our hearts and God can still hear us through The Holy Spirit. That is marvellous isn't it? However, He has given each of us a voice and He does love to hear our voice because it is special and different from each others.

Psalm: 106 verse 48   Dec 31

Praise be to The LORD, the God of Israel, from everlasting to everlasting. Let all the people say, "Amen".

Well this is the last day of the year and tomorrow we shall be able God willing to be praising Him at the start of a brand NEW YEAR. So I want to say, God bless you for sharing with me throughout this year that that has just gone and hope that you may like to start afresh in the New Year with me praising Almighty God, Our Father in Heaven, with Jesus Christ our Saviour and The Holy spirit. I pray for wonderful blessings for us all in the year that is coming as we walk together praising and worshipping our God who reigns for ever and ever with myriads and myriads of Angels surrounding Him and the great cloud of witnesses above. Amen. Amen Amen.

***

Scripture quotations are taken from the HOLY BIBLE, NEW INTERNATIONAL VERSION.

Copyright © 1973, 1978, 1984 by International Bible Society

Also: From the Authorised King James Version

.....

©
Copyright of this Book
Drink from the Cup Writings
&
Illustrations belong to the Author Jessie M.R. Larman

www.ingramcontent.com/pod-product-compliance
Lightning Source LLC
Chambersburg PA
CBHW050636300426
44112CB00012B/1822